EXPLORING BRITAIN'S CANALS

EXPLORING BRITAIN'S CANALS

PAUL ATTERBURY

Photography by Ian Burgum

Introduction by
TIMOTHY WEST AND PRUNELLA SCALES

HarperCollins*Publishers*

First published in 1994 by HarperCollins *Publishers,* London

Main text © Paul Atterbury 1994
Introduction text © Timothy West and Prunella Scales 1994
Photographs and maps © Julian Holland Publishing Ltd 1994

The Authors assert the moral right to be identified as the authors of this work

A CIP catalogue record for this book is available from the British Library

ISBN 0 00 218534-2

Designed and conceived by Julian Holland Publishing Ltd, Somerset UK
Feature photography by Ian Burgum
Edited by Sue Gordon
Typesetting and page make-up by Henry Buckton
Cartography by Gecko Ltd

Printed and bound in Italy

Acknowledgements
We would like to thank the following individuals and companies for supplying additional photography for pages 172-92:

Paul Atterbury, Julian Holland, British Waterways, AA Photo Library.

The author would in addition like to thank Sue Whitaker for making sense of his manuscript.

The photographer would also like to thank the following individuals for their help and co-operation: Mr. & Mrs. Green; Dave Thomas, Boat Builder & Repairer; Mr. Roger Shafi, Clifton Steel; and all canal users, lock and bridge keepers.

Contents

Introduction

WE WERE at a wedding recently, and a lady in white hat and gloves came up and asked had we not made a television programme about the Kennet and Avon Canal? Yes, we admitted. 'I live on the Kennet and Avon Canal,' she told us, 'at Claverton.' A lovely spot, we said. 'It *was*', she said, 'a *lovely* spot. And then they went and put water in the canal, and now I have to watch a lot of boats going past the window.'

Well, you can't please everyone. We ourselves tend to place rather a high value on the provision of water, but that's because we own a boat. Canals offer so many different sorts of recreation: beautiful walks and cycle rides along the towpath, angling, watching the wildlife, discovering history, or just sitting at a lock enjoying the sound and movement of the water.

A canal is quite different from a river. Not simply because one is made by man and the other by God: there is a different feel about canals, particularly in built-up areas. In the nature of things, a town or village springs up around its local river. If in addition there is a canal, because the river is unnavigable or awkward, this tends to be hidden away round the back somewhere. In other words, if the river is a town's natural thoroughfare, the canal is its service road. From the canal, you see England from the back.

There are other differences too, human ones. There is a friendliness, a corporate spirit among canal boaters which is perhaps not characteristic of their counterpart on the river. (If this is an unwarrantable generalisation, then we apologise but stick to our guns – that's how it seems to us.) River people tend to display an appetite for competition, as to the size, appearance and speed of their craft. Chugging along a 15ft channel in a narrow boat at three and a half knots, however, provides little challenge to the competitive spirit.

Yachting caps and blazers are definitely *out* on a canal – woolly hats and Real Ale badges are in, but not compulsory. If you get into trouble on a canal – mechanical, navigational (the technical term for getting stuck in the mud), or personal (falling in) – someone will always lend a helping hand. As they will undoubtedly say, however much your misfortune may have been brought about by your own folly, 'It could happen to anyone'.

Our own boat is a sort of country cottage for us, with the added advantage that if you want to, you can look out of your bedroom window at a different view every morning. We were introduced to canal life 17 years ago by an actress friend, Lynn Farleigh, who owned a half-share in a narrow boat on the Oxford Canal, on which we had a wonderful holiday. Our two sons were aged ten and seven at the time, and got splendidly tired handling locks and bridges, collapsing immediately after supper and leaving their parents free to play chess or scrabble, have a drink and watch the sun go down. Our use of Lynn's boat became so regular that when she announced that she wanted to sell her share of it, we eagerly took up her offer, and only parted with it five years ago when we bought our own 60-footer.

People have their own ideas about the overall design, decoration and equipment of a narrow boat, and these decisions are governed principally by whether you intend to make the boat your permanent home or whether you want to be able to fly to it when you have a spare 24 hours and put it straight into commission. Home boat owners, the serious canal folk, tend usually to go for traditional design – solid fuel stoves, potted plants, oil lamps, buckets and billy-cans painted with canal-art roses, a copper kettle on the black-leaded hearth. Their gestures to the 20th century might include a battery-driven television set, a mobile phone, and a

Opposite: *Traditionally decorated canal boat on the Kennet & Avon Canal near the Caen Hill flight of locks at Devizes.*

Above: *The comfortable interior of a modern narrow boat at Braunston, Grand Union Canal.*

bicycle on the roof. And normally there's a dog. We dilettante part-timers, on the other hand, tend to favour an unashamedly more modern interior – it being important to us to get the fridge working (and the central heating if necessary), cook a meal and get under way without too much loss of time, and at the end of the trip, to get round the boat with a mop and dustpan and brush as easily as possible. On the other hand, the television and the portable phone might just be the things you're most glad to get away from.

Sixty feet seems a lot of boat, especially when you're steering it, from the stern, for the first time. Our previous boat was 48ft long, and our friend Barry Morse of Banbury, building our new one, persuaded us to go the extra 12 feet. We're very glad he did. There's a bit more room everywhere, but the most important improvement is that the double bed is permanent; it doesn't have to be reconstructed out of the dining table every evening, an exercise so complicated and exhausting at the end of a hard day's sailing that we used to put it off and put it off, waking cold and stiff at four in the

morning still bent over the table. With an additional four single bunks at the stern, and the settee, we can berth up to seven people; any more than that in a 60ft narrow boat, and everybody has to know each other very well indeed.

In this country we seem to have a great aptitude for rescuing doomed artefacts at the 11th hour and 59th minute. When private groups of volunteers started taking over abandoned railway lines in the 1950s, renovating them and putting them back into service, the cynics declared the practice to be no more than a passing enthusiasm, bound to spread itself thinner and thinner as more and more such exercises were carried out all over the country, until it perished of over-expansion. They were of course quite wrong. There are now a score of reclaimed railways, and the number is still growing. It is the same with the British canals. At the same time as the engineer and author Tom Rolt led off the railway rescue movement with the salvation of the Tal-y-llyn narrow gauge line in Merioneth, he and his confrères were also working to save the recently closed Kennet and Avon Canal from the permanent abandonment sought by Parliament. It ran 87 miles across England from east to west, linking the Thames with the Bristol Avon. A lot of it had already drained away, and developers were awaiting the green light to start building over its track. During the next four decades pressure was brought to bear on the government, an Association (later a Trust) was formed, money was raised and engineering work was carried out, largely using voluntary labour, on a colossal scale. When this incredible feat of restoration was accomplished in 1900, we helped HTV make a film about the re-opening, and as we sailed the first boat along the canal for 39 years, it was impossible to suppress an unusual glow of national pride.

Now there are canal reclamation schemes going on all over the place: the Wiltshire and Berkshire, the Rochdale in the Pennines, the Wey and Arun Navigation, which used to carry barges from the Thames at Weybridge down to Littlehampton and out into the English Channel, saving about 100 miles by not going through London and the Thames Estuary. And there are various others too. Britain once had the most intricate network of canals in the world but, interestingly, commercial traffic even in its heyday was never as heavy as the still growing volume of pleasure craft today.

Let us not, however, give you the impression that canals are overcrowded, or that your boat will find itself snarled up in a traffic jam trying to get through the next lock. On a fine August Sunday on the Grand Union, you might find yourself wishing there were somewhat fewer people about, but mostly you can count on pottering along for miles without meeting a living soul. Except the odd fisherman, who in all probability will not return your greeting.

If you're hiring a boat for a holiday, think carefully about which canal you fancy. Each canal is different. That's not just a platitude, it's true. Every canal was built for a specific purpose, to handle a certain kind of traffic, had its own kind of terrain to conquer and employed its own forms of engineering to do this. The personality of the canal engineer, the history of its construction, and its subsequent good or ill fortune all leave their mark. We seem to have visited most of the waterways described in these pages at one time or another, as well as one or two extra ones, but there are probably enough to keep us going for the remainder of our lives.

The Kennet and Avon we've already mentioned. It's a very beautiful canal, especially at its western end. There are two fine aqueducts and many lovely bridges, but the most dramatic feature of the canal is the Caen Hill flight of 29 locks – 16 of them in a single 'staircase'. When we arrived for the re-opening as first boat up the flight of brand-new locks, we had a great deal of assistance from the British Waterways Board personnel, who I think were as nervous as we were. Maintaining water levels was a problem, and a certain amount of discreet ramming to open the top gates was quietly

advised. We've been up the flight since, and nowadays things are arranged so that you go up two abreast, with another pair of boats waiting to follow you into the lock you've just left. This is to save water, and means you have an easier time of it, but it still feels like a good morning's work, and you're happy to get to the pub at the top of the flight, which, as you can imagine, does a roaring trade.

This saving of water is a very important consideration. Passage up and down Caen Hill is often limited to two days a week, so that the greatest possible number of craft can share the water. Every time the flight is used, 11 million gallons of water are released, to flow away westwards down into the Avon and out into the Bristol Channel, so obviously it doesn't make sense to do this for just one boat. The K & A is in fact rather a peculiar canal in this respect. Because the money ran out when John Rennie was building it, the summit of the canal was much shorter than he'd intended – only three and a half miles to feed

Below: The Kennet & Avon Canal at Bathampton on the final approach to Bath.

Above: *Late evening fishing at Cadley bridge, Wootton Top, on the Kennet & Avon Canal.*

Opposite: *Boats negotiating Bank Newton locks on the Leeds & Liverpool Canal.*

busy commercial route, and there are one or two traditional canal villages, like Thrupp, with a pretty terrace of cottages strung along the towpath. Thrupp was where our seven-year old son Joe fell in, clutching in each hand a heavy windlass for operating lock sluices, and, although already a good swimmer, sank to the bottom. As we were preparing to rescue him, he came up a second time but immediately disappeared again, and we remembered the stern instruction we had given: Never, *never* let go of the windlass; if you lose it, you're done for. 'Let go, you idiot,' we shouted, 'We'd rather have *you*.' Reluctantly, he relinquished his grasp, re-surfaced and we fished him out. Some wonderful man appeared with one of those powerful magnets on a rope, sank it into the water and eventually came up with both the windlasses. He owned a wooden-hulled horsedrawn barge, and introduced us to the horse. We asked if the horse enjoyed his life on the towpath. 'What he really loves', said his owner, 'is trampling on anglers.'

Everybody falls in at some time or other – but if you can't swim, try not to do it in a lock. Locks are deep, by definition, but the cruiseway of most canals is likely to be only three or four feet in depth, and unless you're unlucky enough to stand on a piece of broken glass or sharp metal that some idiot has thrown into the water, you're not likely to come to any harm. Quite a few canals, indeed, are very pleasant to swim in (but don't risk it in Birmingham).

The Oxford in fact goes on beyond the Grand Union and continues northward to Hawkesbury Junction, where it joins the Coventry Canal. Another, smaller ring that you could do in a week takes you up to Tamworth, along the Trent and Mersey Canal east to Shardlow, and down the Grand Union again through Leicester, back to where you started. We once did this as far as Shardlow, but then continued north through Nottingham because we had a fancy eventually to get up to the Leeds and Liverpool Canal – we were both about to work in Yorkshire for a spell. There

another 84 miles with water from a single reservoir. An appeal has been launched to provide for back-pumping, which really is essential for such a popular waterway.

All canals, however, are liable to suffer when there's a drought – we ran aground in the shallows for a whole day on the Oxford Canal once, discovering later that a local farmer had been drilling holes in the bank and tapping off the water for his potato crop. When we finally prised ourselves free, we passed a poor man whose hired boat had stuck fast five hours after he took it out. He seemed destined to spend his whole holiday in the shadow of Banbury Station.

The Oxford is really our Alma Mater, a more modest piece of work than the K & A, but very attractive, and very useful to holiday boaters because it forms part of a navigable ring. If you start at Brentford, for instance, you can go up the Thames and on to the canal at Oxford, join the Grand Union at Napton Junction and thence go all the way down to Brentford again. It was once a

Above: *Negotiating Bosley locks on the Macclesfield Canal.*

are basically two ways of getting up into the splendid waterways of the north. Either you keep to the west of the Pennines by going through the Potteries, through water that looks exactly like tomato soup, up the pretty little Macclesfield Canal and through Manchester, or you take the easterly route, down the River Trent.

Now, the Trent is tidal for much of the way, and negotiating a tidal river in a narrow boat needs quite a bit of careful thought. There are over 40 miles of tidal Trent before you turn off west on to the Stainforth and Keadby Canal, and of course you cannot travel that distance in a single day. To pass the night moored in tidal water you need riding lights and an anchor, and we don't carry either. However, 30 miles along the tidal way, near Gainsborough, is the entrance to the Chesterfield

Canal. It's a dead end, but you can nip in there through the lock and take shelter for the night. Obviously you have to start at first light, but you also have to study your tide tables. If the tide's coming in, you've got the current against you and you'll probably never make it; if it's going out, then well and good, but even so you have to time things so that the tide's still in when you get to Gainsborough or there won't be enough water to get you over the cill and into the lock. Quite exciting.

We went along the River Ouse to York, and on up the Ure to Ripon, or nearly to Ripon, because this promising-looking little canal comes to an undignified halt where someone has thoughtlessly thrown over it a road bridge so low that navigation beyond is impossible, and it peters out in disgust.

Ripon is the furthest north you can get without craning your boat out of the water and carrying it by road. We returned through York and Selby, leaving the boat in the centre of Leeds for a couple of weeks (where there is now a splendid Canal Basin development) and then continuing along the Leeds and Liverpool. This canal is much more beautiful than its name might suggest: 127 miles from one city to the other, climbing past factories and mills into open pasture land, through woods and out along the side of green hills becoming gradually more rugged until you reach the wild moorland and distant mountains of the summit, then gradually down through a remote countryside and into the Foulridge tunnel (nearly a mile long with no towpath) before descending to the cobbled backstreets, the disused wharves and warehouses of Nelson, Burnley, Blackburn and on to Wigan and the cultivated Lancashire lowlands.

Foulridge tunnel has its own legend. In 1912 a cow fell into the canal just by the south entrance, and for some reason decided to swim through the tunnel. Pulled out the other end, she was revived with alcohol. The animal's adventure is photographically commemorated in the local pub.

By the way, wear a coat and hat whenever you go through a tunnel – the roof is liable to drip heavily. We once repainted the top of our boat on a cloudless summer day, convinced of the impossibility of rain, and then went straight into a tunnel; our work was wrecked in moments. The experience can be exciting, though, especially when, in a 'broad' tunnel with (just) enough room for craft to pass one another, you see a boat coming in the opposite direction at what appears, in the pitch dark, to be about 30 miles an hour.

Being able to visit the boat for only a few days at a time between engagements, we got into the habit of leaving it either at a secure boatyard or at a mooring where some kind resident boatperson

Right: *Boat leaving the lowest of the five staircase locks at Bingley on the Leeds & Liverpool Canal.*

could keep a neighbourhood watch until we returned in a week or two to pick it up and move on elsewhere. We've only been burgled twice. Once two schoolboys in Wellingborough asked us if they could come on board to look at the boat, had some lemonade, thanked us politely and went off with rather a good camera. On another occasion we returned after a fortnight away to find the lock had been picked, half a bottle of our whisky had been consumed, and a jug and two glasses had been washed up and left tidily on the draining board. Other people have not been so fortunate, and it really is worth paying a little for the security of a boatyard that's locked at night.

Using your boat peripatetically like this does mean you can go further afield than you ever could without devoting three months at a stretch to the exploration of the canal network. Before making our gradual way down south again, we wanted to see the Llangollen Canal. This delightful canal is very narrow, very shallow, and very popular – so popular indeed that at weekends at the height of the season it's impossible to enjoy what essentially is a quiet, meandering stream. Quiet though it is, it boasts one of the most majestic constructions on the whole canal system – Thomas Telford's Pontcysyllte aqueduct. Boats can travel in single file along the 1,000ft iron trough that contains the water. There is a slim towpath on the east side, with a railing. Don't look out on the opposite side if you suffer from vertigo, because there is nothing between you and the Dee Valley 120ft below except the narrow lip of the iron trough, just beneath the level of your deck. To add to the unnerving experience, the whole trough tends to throb and shake to the rhythm of your engine. Crew members sometimes choose this moment to feel rather tired and need to lie down on their bunks below.

We could go on rhapsodising about various canals we've travelled and still mean to travel – the

Right: *Flying across the Dee Valley on the 120ft high Pontcysyllte Aqueduct, Llangollen Canal.*

Grand Union, with its various little interesting branches; the Aire and Calder, still commercially used; the scenically exciting Shropshire Union, and perhaps the best of all the 'ring' journeys, from Stratford-on-Avon down the river to Tewkesbury, up the Severn to Worcester, on the Worcester and Birmingham Canal to King's Norton Junction and down the charming little Stratford-on-Avon Canal to the basin just beside the Royal Shakespeare Theatre. But you will read about most of these more fully and much more informatively in the following pages. We've just tried to describe to you some of the pleasure we've had from what we still think of as probably the best buy of our lives – our canal boat.

One last word of probably needless advice to those who are contemplating sailing the canals for the first time. Don't hurry. Life at 3mph can be good. Don't make plans necessitating your reaching a certain place by a certain time. If you do that, you'll always find there was a pretty walk you didn't have time for, or a country church you'd like to have looked at, or an attractive canalside pub you had to pass by. You might want to stop just to look at a heron, or because you thought you'd glimpsed the swoop of a kingfisher. Just get to wherever you are when you want to stop. And curiously enough, you'll always have the sensation of achievement, of having travelled hard and got somewhere else, even if you could have done it in half an hour in the car. Go by canal, and you stretch the country.

And if anything should go wrong, remember that you can always walk there quicker.

Prunella Scales
Timothy West

October 1993

The Monmouthshire and Brecon Canal

MY FIRST experience of the canal still familiarly, if incorrectly, known as the Mon & Brec was in the late 1960s, when its then unnavigable 33 miles made an excellent, and rather energetic weekend walk. When walking one travels at roughly the same speed as a boat, which means the leisurely enjoyment of the canal and its landscape is much the same. The only real difficulty with canal walking, apart from the occasionally erratic nature of some towpaths, is how to get there and then, if you are not to retrace your steps, how to get back. Travelling to the canal by car is generally the best option but, unless there is a friend prepared to meet you at the other end, you finish the walk tired but triumphant, and a long way from your car. Quite often unpredictable buses and expensive taxis are the only way to get back to the beginning, and a difficult journey to recover the car can undermine the pleasures of the walk with surprising rapidity. On occasions I have been driven to hitchhike, a means of travel completely without the appeal it seemed to have when young and feckless. Another option is to involve a bicycle in some way, perhaps leaving it at the end of the walk first and then driving back to the starting point. This was fine in the old days, but today the chances of the bicycle still being there, in one piece, to greet one's arrival seem pretty remote.

The best canal walks are those planned in conjunction with trains. For obvious engineering reasons, many canals have railways that follow their route, and so walks can be planned with stations, and train services, at both ends. Sometimes there are intermediate stops as well, very useful if

A quiet evening mooring near Llangynidr locks, with autumn colours showing the Mon & Brec at its best.

The Monmouthshire and Brecon Canal

From Pontymoile Junction, near Pontypool, to Brecon
33 miles long, with 6 locks

Notable features Pontymoile Junction, the Rogerstone or Cefu flight of 14 locks on the Crumlin branch of the old Monmouthshire Canal, Goytre wharf and limekilns, Govilon, Gilwern, Llangattock and Talybont wharves and the routes of their tramways, easily explored on foot, Abergavenny and Crickhowell, Llangynidr locks, Ashford tunnel, Brecon. Plus the landscape of the Usk Valley and the Brecon Beacons, an eternally changing towpath panorama.

History In 1793 parliamentary assent was given for a canal, to be called the Brecknock and Abergavenny, to link Brecon with the River Usk near Newport. The scheme, promoted by local businessmen and landowners, was designed to improve and cheapen the transport of coal, lime, agricultural produce and domestic wares. Originally it was planned quite independently of its southern neighbour, the Monmouthshire Canal, which was to link Newport and the Severn with the rapidly industrialising valleys of the Ebbw and the Usk. In the event the two schemes came together, and the promoters of the Brecknock and Abergavenny changed their route to allow an end-to-end junction with the Monmouthshire at Pontymoile. Work began in 1797, under the control of the engineer Thomas Dadford, and it was he who determined the eccentric lock size of 63ft by 9ft, a dimension associated only with the canals of South Wales and reflecting their independence from the national network. The Monmouthshire Canal, with 42 locks in its two branches to Crumlin and Pontymoile, was opened in 1796, but its northern partner was much slower in building. Completed in stages from Brecon southwards, the Brecknock and Abergavenny did not finally reach Pontymoile until 1812. Although linked together, the two canals were commercial rivals for a long period, and the Brecknock and Abergavenny often had the edge, thanks to its lower toll rates. Colliery owners and ironmasters constructed a network of horsedrawn tramways to bring their products down to the wharves along the canal, and soon it was the backbone of an extensive network that ensured its success and prosperity until the 1850s. Increasing railway competition and the greater use of imported iron ores forced the two canals to merge in 1865, and then in 1880 the whole undertaking was bought by the Great Western Railway and renamed the Monmouthshire and Brecon Canal. Trade diminished steadily through the last decades of the 19th century, and by the 1920s the canals were kept alive only by limited local cargoes. The tramways closed or were absorbed by railways, and by the 1930s commercial traffic was at an end. From then on the canals gently declined, and both were closed in the early 1960s. The Monmouthshire remained closed, and much of its route became permanently unusable, but the Brecon and Abergavenny remained largely intact, frozen in time. In 1968 a full restoration project started and by 1970 the canal was ready to play its part in the new leisure revolution that was giving canals an unexpected lease of life.

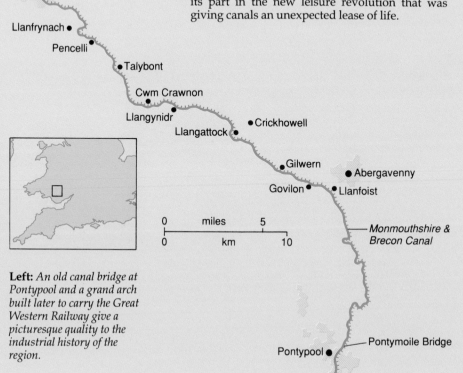

Left: *An old canal bridge at Pontypool and a grand arch built later to carry the Great Western Railway give a picturesque quality to the industrial history of the region.*

one is overcome by exhaustion or driven to despair by rain. Unfortunately, the Mon & Brec is not in this rather desirable category. In fact, it offers the worst of all worlds, namely a railway connection at one end, the southern, but no way of travelling from there to anywhere remotely useful, least of all to Brecon, at the northern end, whose rail links were firmly severed during the Beeching years.

Back in the 1960s the Mon & Brec was a rather private and little known waterway, lying dormant in a semi-derelict state, having been quietly abandoned, if not officially closed, for some decades. The last recorded commercial traffic on the canal was in 1933. Very limited boating was still possible in some sections, and much of the canal was in water, but dropped bridges, broken locks and considerable silting from years of neglect made serious navigation quite impossible. The isolated position the canal enjoyed, deep in the heart of South Wales and miles from any other waterway, also made the Mon & Brec into a kind of sleeping beauty. What I did not know at the time was that it was about to be kissed into life again by the new fervour for canal restoration, then about to sweep across the country. By 1970 the Mon & Brec had undergone a complete overhaul, thanks to the efforts of various bodies, including the British Waterways Board, as it then was, the local authorities along its route, the Brecon Beacons National Park, and the many volunteers keen to spend their spare time up to their knees in mud. Boats were once again able to travel from Pontypool to Brecon via some of the most attractive scenery on the British canal network. Hire bases and all the other paraphernalia of the canal leisure industry soon followed, but the Mon & Brec was able to absorb the onslaught and retain its particular appeal. Once again, it was its isolation that saved it, for on the Mon & Brec a boat can only cruise slowly from one end to the other and back

Right: *A narrow boat steerer carefully lines his craft up to pass under the Penawr lift bridge, raised by a crew member.*

again, a leisurely activity easily undertaken within a one-week hire period. Most people, therefore, come here once, cruise it thoroughly, cross it off the list, and move on to more expansive waterways. Only those who really love it come back for a second go, and then they tend to return again and again, drawn back by the enduring attractions of what is not only one of the prettiest canals in Britain, but also one of our best-kept waterway secrets.

Hard to grasp today is the *raison d'être* for this lovely canal that makes its quiet way through delightful scenery from nowhere in particular to a small market town in the Brecon Beacons National Park. The canal mania of the late 18th century produced some amazingly bizarre and impractical schemes, some of which actually got well past the drawing board and into the ample pockets of the willing speculators, but today, even with this historical background in mind, it is difficult to imagine people queuing up to invest their savings in the Mon & Brec. Yet they did, the canal was built,

and for some decades it proved to be a highly profitable enterprise. It is a perfect example of a British canal, fully equipped with locks, aqueducts, lift bridges, old wharves and even a tunnel, and with a delightfully meandering course underlining the particular way that 18th-century canal engineers saved money by making their waterways stick rigidly, whenever possible, to one contour line. Easily appreciated as a living example of canal history, the Mon & Brec has, beneath its rural façade, a lively commercial background that is not immediately apparent from its wandering route through a gentle landscape.

In its day, the canal was at the very heart of the Industrial Revolution in South Wales, a vital artery for the coal and iron that fuelled the furnaces of industrialisation. Conceived in the early 1790s, and then built in stages between 1797 and 1812, the Brecknock & Abergavenny Canal, as it was then called, was paid for entirely by local people. A huge investment despite its careful planning and economical construction by the engineer Thomas Dadford, the canal was soon repaying the hopes of its supporters. By the 1820s it was highly successful, its boats carrying hundreds of thousands of tons of coal, iron ore, iron, limestone, lime, agricultural produce and a wide range of general commercial and domestic cargoes. The secrets of its success lay partly in the route, from Brecon southwards to the junction with the Monmouthshire Canal at Pontymoile, and thus to Newport with its busy docks, ironworks and fatories, but also in the horsedrawn tramways that connected with the canal. Nearly 200 miles of these brought the raw materials of industry from the quarries, collieries and furnaces up in the hills down to six wharves spread along the route, at Brecon, Talybont, Llangattock, Gilwern, Govilon and Llanfoist. For over 40 years the Brecknock and Abergavenny Canal was crucial to the economic development of the region, serving the needs of both industry and agriculture. During this period it must have presented to any visitor a turmoil of activity, with

the comings and goings of the wagons on their primitive iron railways, and a steady stream of boats, all horsedrawn like the wagons, working their way up and down a canal whose surroundings were limekilns and furnaces, quarries and pits instead of today's landscape of native woodland and peaceful hillsides.

The decline started in the 1860s with the railways taking, year by year, more and more of the canal's traffic, and by the end of the century all that remained were the local agricultural cargoes. The pattern of decline was matched by changes in ownership. In 1865 the Brecknock & Abergavenny was sold to its rival and trading partner, the Monmouthshire Canal. Fifteen years later the whole network was taken over, as with so many other canals, by railway companies. It was its new railway owner, the Great Western, who renamed the canal the Monmouthshire and Brecon, and ironically it is this name that has stuck, albeit in the shortened form of Mon & Brec. Today the name lingers on, even though the restored canal is entirely the former Brecon (or Brecknock) & Abergavenny, with virtually none of the Monmouthshire, whose scattered remains are permanently abandoned.

The Mon & Brec is predominantly a canal for all seasons, with the colours of its landscape and the trees that line the banks for much of the route offering a changing spectacle through the year. The surrounding woodland, of alder, beech, oak, ash, sycamore and other familiar native species, is largely natural, and is full of birds and flowers. It is a good canal for heron and kingfisher-spotting, thanks to the isolation and the limited boat traffic, and its surroundings represent an ideal vision of the British countryside, with all the flora and fauna generally considered to be essential elements in such a setting. It has its surprises, some of them unpleasant such as the mink, that nasty little

Left: *The river-like quality of the canal near Llanfrynach shows how well it takes its place in the landscape.*

predator that destroys everything it meets, and some of them unexpected. Walking along one day and hearing a frantic splashing and thrashing, I looked across to the opposite bank to see a duck locked in apparently mortal combat with a large eel. The writhing contours of the eel gave the scene a curiously classical quality, with echoes of Laocoön and the serpents. The drama continued until the duck got the upper hand, but the causes of the conflict were never clear. A canal is always a good place for the unusual, mainly because the slow pace of life gives ample opportunity for the observation of incidents and trifles that would normally be missed.

With time on my hands during a recent visit to Newport, I decided to take a look at the old Monmouthshire Canal. I knew that trying to find its remains in the centre of Newport would be a waste of time, its route having been totally obliterated by roads and other recent development. However, I did find on the walls of a pedestrian underpass somewhere near the castle a fine series of recent murals depicting the former industrial life of the town, and among the docks and railway locomotives there were some carefully presented studies of canal boats. The best place to start my exploration seemed to be near Barrack Hill, where its famous Crumlin branch swung westwards away from the main line, a point now overshadowed by the M4 motorway. Thanks to the improvements and environmental tidying up carried out in recent years, it is now possible to follow the canal along official towpath walkways, routes widely enjoyed by joggers, mountain bicyclists and a steady stream of elderly people with dogs.

A recent addition, not far from the motorway crossing, is a fully restored lock, in working order. While interesting, and perhaps popular with walkers and visiting parties of schoolchildren, this does seem rather a folly. Below it the canal soon peters out, and will certainly never be navigable again, while above it a short walk leads to a new road bridge much too low for boats and a flight of

long disused locks, cascaded as a series of waterfalls. Here is a lock, expensively restored with money that could usefully have been spent on many a practical restoration project, that will never be used by anything bigger than a canoe. It does not even have a surrounding theme park to justify it. The full restoration of the Monmouthshire to a navigable canal south from Pontypool to this point is a theoretical possibility, and a dream no doubt cherished by local enthusiasts. But how many boaters would seriously want to work their way down a long flight of locks, knowing that at the end there was little more than a good view of the M4 and the hard work of climbing back up the same locks? Sometimes in our insatiable desire to re-create the past we lose all sense of proportion.

Above: *Following its contour line, the canal winds along the hillside north of Pencelli.*

Following the Monmouthshire on the carefully tended towpath walkways north through Cwmbran to Pontypool is a pleasant enough but not very exciting experience. Before the current burst of enthusiasm for restoration and linear walkways, following any towpath was quite an adventurous activity, full of all kinds of uncertainties. Sometimes the towpath would disappear altogether, either sunk into the canal or made impassable by both natural and man-made obstacles. Progress was often hindered by overgrown and generally thorny bushes, fallen trees and the occasional mad dog. There always seemed to be plenty of mud. Abandoned pieces of domestic equipment were encountered in the most unexpected and remote spots, and one could only wonder at the immense effort that had been expended to get them there. Dumping large and heavy items in inaccessible places must represent some kind of a challenge. Penetrating decayed urban sections of canals ran the risk of assault by rampant hooligans or aggressive fishermen, while country stretches were often so isolated that anyone immobilised by a broken ankle or some other unexpected disaster might have had to wait for days before being rescued.

A far better walk than the Monmouthshire's northbound towpath is up its Crumlin branch, a canal that climbs for 9 miles into that part of South Wales, known, with no particular relevance, as Little Switzerland. This was Victorian enterprise at its best, a canal thrown up a steep valley with 19 locks – 14 of which are in one dramatic flight that raised it 168ft – and built almost regardless of cost. For a culture that cannot even decide to build a proper rail link for the Channel Tunnel, such behaviour must be unthinkable. Yet in its day the Crumlin branch was both busy and profitable, providing precisely the kind of transport infrastructure that was to ensure the successful development of the surrounding region. The canal remained in use until the 1930s and then was finally abandoned in 1962, but it remains in reasonable

Above: *The art of traditional canal painting demonstrated by the Buckby can, or water container, on the* Rose of Brecon *at Govilon.*

Below: *A modern inland navigator, the proud owner of the narrow boat* Tramp *at Gilwern.*

order, extensively tidied up by the local authority and as a result makes a most enjoyable and instructive walk. You can visit the Fourteen Lock Canal Centre right by the first of the Rogerstone locks.

When the Monmouthshire Canal was at its peak, its main line served a valley filled with the noise, smoke and smells associated with an industry that made things from metal. Tinplate was the mainstay of the Pontypool region, bringing both wealth and squalor to a hitherto rural river valley. Today, this industry is, like its canal, a piece of history. The canal survives as a kind of ghost, but of tinplating there is no trace, and all the products of this once extensive industry are in museums or antique shops. Its route is surrounded by that characteristic late 20th-century New Town landscape of completely indifferent architecture, with little to choose between factories and housing estates. For this reason, most people quite sensibly head straight for Pontymoile Junction, an interesting place where the Brecon & Abergavenny starts its journey northwards. Old cottages and bridges, the still discernible routes of former tramways and railways, and a stop lock where tolls were once collected from boats passing from one canal to another all bring it to life. This is also officially the southern limit of the navigable section, although boaters wishing to penetrate a bit further into the pleasures of a modern urban landscape can do so.

The particular quality of the Mon & Brec is soon apparent, for its route takes it quickly away from modern development and into the striking landscape of the Usk Valley and the surrounding peaks of the Brecon Beacons. Its contour route, high in the hillside and hidden from views by trees, is soon established. From the canal itself, the views are continuously exciting as peak after peak comes into sight, framed by the trees, and towering over a valley of green fields, woodland, farms and churches. There is plenty of canal interest, with a choice of old canal buildings, a great variety of bridges and, for the addict, a good range of original cast iron mile posts surviving in the undergrowth. A feature of the canal is the old wharves, today generally centres of boating activity. Limekilns and old warehouses at these now remote spots hint at a very different past. Goytre and Llanfoist may seem delightfully rural but a century and a half ago they were teeming with an activity in which leisure played no part at all. From the wharf at Llanfoist there was a tramway to the ironworks up in the hills at Blaenavon. Opened in about 1825, it left the canal via a tunnel and then climbed steeply via four inclined planes, down which wagons loaded with iron used to hurtle. These tramways, pioneering routes that launched the railway age in Britain, were the crude but essential backbone upon which the industrial wealth of the region was built, and at their heart was the canal. The route today can easily be explored on foot, and those with sharp eyes will find, both here and on other tramways, surviving examples of the stone sleeper blocks that carried the iron rails. To the east, across the Usk, and about a mile away, is Abergavenny, a town that gave its name to a canal that never came near it.

To the west of Llanfoist is the site of a major breach. Here in 1975 the canal bank gave way and a whole section was swept into the valley below, a tidal wave of mud and debris that cleared away all the trees in its path. The scar can still be seen. Always a risk with canals on embankments or cut into the sides of hills, breaches are a part of history and folklore. Some famous ones, such as that at Prestolee on the Manchester, Bolton and Bury, closed their canals for ever, but generally repairs were made. On rare occasions boats were carried into the breach, but more often they simply found themselves suddenly sitting on the muddy bed of an empty canal. There are many things that cause a breach, from inadequate or careless building in the first place to subsidence provoked by drought, flooding or even excessive burrowing of rabbits.

Attractive wharfs are also to be found at Govilon and Gilwern, another area rich in old iron and coal tramway routes. Some of these were later absorbed

Above: *Built along traditional lines, the modern hire boats of the Beacon Park fleet at Llanfoist wharf offer their crews a comfortable introduction to the delights of canal cruising.*

into the network of railways that ultimately drove the canals out of business. Ironically, most of these have in their turn closed and largely disappeared, leaving the canal as the unexpected winner in the transport history stakes. Some of the wharves have near them that other characteristic feature of the Mon & Brec, the drain plug. When the canal was built, it had in its bed a series of drain holes with fitted iron covers, designed to facilitate maintenance. Originally these were connected by a length of chain to a windlass on the towpath but inevitably the locations of some of these, both on this and on other canals, were forgotten in the mists of time. There have, as a result, been occasions when modern maintenance men, giving a hefty pull on a length of old chain found on the canal bed, have been surprised to find themselves in a rapidly emptying canal.

The route along, and above, the Usk Valley is particularly attractive, past Crickhowell and the old weaving village of Llangattock, and with lovely views of the eastern peaks, notably Sugar Loaf and Table Mountain. The section through the Dardy is probably the best, a visual treat in the golden light of early evening. At Llangynidr traditional canal engineering reasserts itself, in the form of a flight of delightfully placed locks, and an aqueduct over the Afon Crawnon. Then comes the short (375yd) Ashford tunnel, its entrance looking little bigger than a drainage culvert. Small, rocky and with a dangerously undulating roof that has given many a boater a sore head, the tunnel has neither towpath nor passing space, and so the towing horses took the path across the top as usual in such cases. Talybont has another old wharf, built to serve the 12-mile long Bryn Oer tramway that from 1815 brought coal down to the canal. Just to the north is another rarity, a modern electrically operated lift

Left: *A variety of canal craft moored at Llangattock wharf, below the rounded summit of Craig y Cilau.*

Right: *Looking up the lock flight at Llangynidr; a boat waits in the chamber for the bottom gates to be closed.*

Above: *The electrically operated lift bridge near Talybont, with the gates used by crew members to stop traffic while the bridge is raised.*

Opposite: *The peaks of the Brecon Beacons form a spectacular setting for the canal near Llanfrynach, with Cambrian Cruisers' base and marina half hidden among the trees.*

and slowly disappearing into the undergrowth, all echoes of a past, or rather a range of pasts. During the summer you can take a trip in a horsedrawn canal boat, a silent glide through the brown waters and the green fields behind the gently muffled hoof beats, another escape into a past of the imagination. Wales is perhaps the country for the imaginary escaper, the traditional centre for alternative living, and the canal is a necessary part of this, along with the craft shops and the National Park.

The last lock before Brecon underlines this theme, a pretty setting with goats wandering around on the towpath, and chickens and ducks scattering through the hedge. Is this really what Wales was like before the Industrial Revolution brought all the muck and noise and wealth, a rural backwater scraping a living any old how? This is certainly the image promoted by the Tourist Information Centre in Brecon, an ugly modern building by the livestock market filled with leaflets about all the escapist things visitors can do.

The canal comes into Brecon beside a busy road, but screened by trees from the worst excesses of the traffic, in summer grinding nose-to-tail. The end comes suddenly, an abrupt stop outside the town just where the fields end and the houses begin, mooring rings surrounded by well-kept grass, litter bins, a childrens' playground, and a notice or two. It is as though the canal builders just gave up. The reality, different of course, is that the canal originally continued to a large wharf nearer the town, but this section disappeared years ago with the end of commercial traffic. A large and handsome brick warehouse of 1892, marooned among later, lesser buildings like a stranded whale, marks the site of the basin. It is only a short walk to the centre of Brecon, a pleasant market town, an elegant centre of old-fashioned shops and tired cafés, the kind of place no longer certain where it belongs. The future is unsure, the past beckons, and so it sits, in between, uncomfortably dealing with a difficult present. On a wall in a quiet street someone has written *'Terry Waite is Clark Kent'*.

bridge carrying a minor road over the canal. These can be found on a number of canals and, like this one, are generally controlled by boaters, whose craft in any case have a right of way. Dropping the gates and lifting the bridge holds up the traffic and gives both pleasure and a great sense of power, as well as establishing the correct order of things. There are one or two such bridges on canals elsewhere that carry roads which at certain times of day become quite busy. A well-timed boat, passing slowly through such a bridge, can cause a most satisfactory traffic jam, with lines of irate and gesticulating motorists forced to wait on both sides of the canal. Also to be found north of Talybont is a series of the more traditional manual lift bridges, built originally to allow farmers to reach fields cut by the canal.

It is easy to understand the appeal of the Mon & Brec. It is a perfect escape, without being demanding, in a lovely landscape, and with the past always apparent. Talybont itself is a village that maintains the illusion. Old petrol pumps, the overgrown track of the closed railway, a field of abandoned VW beetles, moribund, dismembered

PLACES TO VISIT

Abergavenny: traditional market town circled by hills and mountains including Sugar Loaf (1,955ft, easy access from car parks on northwest outskirts); castle remains; Castle and District Museum for local history etc.

Blaenavon: Big Pit Mining Museum, try life as a South Wales miner, descend 300ft shaft, see baths, changing rooms and miner's cottage.

Brecon: attractive old market town, touring centre for the Brecon Beacons; crafts and antique shops, cathedral built mainly in the 13th century, consecrated 1920s; Brecknock Museum has pre-Roman to medieval archaeology, Welsh kitchen, lovespoons etc.

Brecon Beacons National Park: Information Centre at 6 Glamorgan Street, Brecon; walks up into hills from towpath in several places and from nearby roads.

Caerleon, 2 miles N of Newport: impressive baths, barracks and amphitheatre that catered for 6,000 Roman soldiers in the AD75 fortress of Isca (Cadw).

Crickhowell: small, elegant town on far side of 13-arch, medieval stone bridge; former Welsh flannel-making centre and market town with remains of Norman castle.

Gilwern: Bridgend Inn, unpretentious pub with grassy canalside bank.

Llangynidr: Coach and Horses, large old inn with canalside garden, by lowest of the Llangynidr locks.

Newport: The Fourteen Lock Canal Centre, Rogerstone, history of canal, information on locks, canalside walks.

Museum and Art Gallery, local archaeology and history, natural history, paintings, teapot collection.

Tredegar House, splendid 17th-century house, 500 years of life in the Morgan family above and below stairs; boating, adventure playfarm etc.

Pontypool: The Valley Inheritance tells the story of a South Wales valley with exhibits and films.

Tretower Court and Castle: substantial ruins of 11th-century motte and bailey, plus three-storey keep; late 14th-century manor house, in care of Cadw, home of the great 17th-century Welsh poet Henry Vaughan.

The Aire and Calder Canal

ONE OF THE few things that all the great medieval cathedrals and abbeys have in common is their proximity to rivers. At the time of their building, these rivers were vital, providing the only practical means of transporting stone and other materials to the site, not only from local quarries but also from the coastal harbours where imported stone was landed. At this time Britain was covered by a network of rivers that were navigable, up to a point. Traffic would be brought to a halt at times of drought and flood, and there were always battles between boatmen and riverside mill owners over their respective demands upon the limited supplies of water. There were no locks, or other artificial aids to navigation, but sheer practical necessity helped to keep many of the rivers open to traffic. Today, the vast majority of these rivers have long lost any claims to navigable status. Sometimes, standing beside some stream that wanders lazily across a remote field, barely wide or deep enough to float a canoe, it is hard to believe that this was once an active waterway, busy with heavily laden barges.

Yorkshire is a county famous for its abbeys and, not surprisingly, for its variety of rivers. The Ouse, the Don and the Aire, the Calder, the Wharfe and the Hebble, these are among the many waterways that have played their part in the county's history. All were major navigations in the Middle Ages, serving port towns that had grown up well inland, at the top of the tidal flow. Over later centuries, many have ceased to be navigable, either because of physical changes affecting route or water flow, or through the ending of trade. Others, steadily

The dramatic landscape of the Aire and Calder shows the canal and the River Aire with its 18th century bridge dwarfed by the cooling towers of Ferrybridge.

The Aire and Calder Canal

Goole Docks to Leeds City centre
34 miles long, with 12 locks
Branch to Wakefield, 8 miles long with 4 locks
Notable features Goole and its docks, Knottingley and the junction, Ferrybridge power stations and the coal trade, Castleford locks and waterway crossroads, Stanley Ferry aqueduct (Wakefield branch), waterways and basins in Leeds city centre, the distinctive quality of the landscape of East Riding.

History The Aire and the Calder are among the oldest of England's river navigations, and were regularly used by boats from the Middle Ages onwards. However, they were not formally developed into fully fledged navigations, with locks and weirs to control the flow of water, until the very end of the 17th century. By the first decade of the 18th century boats were able to reach Leeds and Wakefield from the rivers Ouse and Humber. The textile trade, particularly the woollen industry, was the first beneficiary, but the export of coal via the new navigations soon became an even more important trade. From the start the Aire and Calder was profitable, and it remained so right up to nationalisation in 1947, thanks largely to the coal industry. As a result, the navigation was constantly improved. The twisting course of the River Aire was bypassed in 1788 by a new canal from Haddlesey to Selby, on the Ouse, and this quickly became a primary route. However, soon the weight of traffic made this waterway too small, and in 1826 a brand new canal was cut from Knottingley to a remote spot on the Ouse, downstream of Selby. Here a new harbour was built, and its accompanying new town of Goole, created from scratch by the canal company, soon became Yorkshire's principal inland port. The Aire and Calder quickly established its prime position as a backbone of a network of very successful canals and river navigations that served the coal trade and allowed the industrial centres of south and east Yorkshire direct access to the major sea ports. Boats were also improved, with the Aire and Calder pioneering a type of compartment boat for the coal trade that could be mechanically loaded and unloaded, and towed by tugs in trains of up to 19 units. Their much larger modern equivalent is still in use, with pusher tugs regularly handling trains of three 170-tonne capacity barges.

The pattern of constant improvement to the waterway has maintained the Aire and Calder and its network as one of the few centres of commercial canal activity in Britain, with oil cargoes now eclipsing coal in importance. The region therefore provides a rare opportunity to see inland waterways still being used for the purpose for which they were originally built some two centuries ago.

Above: *Traditional canal boat painting and lettering at Whitley lock.*

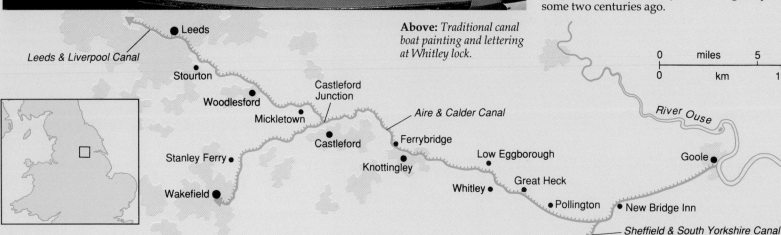

improved, have gradually been absorbed into the national waterway network. Classic examples of the latter are the Aire and the Calder, rivers that have contributed significantly to the industrial and economic development of Yorkshire. It was the needs of the textile trade in Leeds and Wakefield which was the main inspiration for the developments in the late 17th century that turned the Aire and Calder from erratic medieval waterways into a regular navigation. Thanks to the building of locks and weirs, boats were able to reach Leeds by 1700, and Wakefield a few years later. The wool merchants drew immediate benefit from the cheap transport and wider markets these new waterways offered, and they were soon joined by the colliery owners of the hitherto landlocked Yorkshire coalfields. By the middle of the 18th century a flourishing trade had developed, with boats carrying raw wool, limestone and agricultural products upstream, and returning downstream loaded with coal which, believe it or not, was then a major British export. Further improvements were carried out to the waterway between the 1780s and the 1820s, in the form of new canals cut to bypass some of the more tortuous stretches of the River Aire. Links were also established with other navigable rivers of the region, such as the Ouse, and trade continued to expand.

Coal quickly became the backbone of the waterway, and its continued success in the face of railway competition from the middle of the 19th century was due largely to the development of a highly mechanised and efficient coal transport industry. The key to this was that early form of containerisation, the compartment boat. Rather charmingly known as Tom Puddings, these were iron tubs carrying up to 40 tons of coal, and designed to be marshalled into long lines, and then pulled, or later pushed, along by a tug. When first developed by the engineer W H Bartholomew, they were assembled in trains of six, but steady improvements in the technology, plus the increased power of the tugs, brought this total up to 19. The

Tom Puddings were loaded directly from coal staithes with overhead shutes at the collieries, but the real originality of the scheme was at the other end, where they were lifted bodily from the water by giant mechanical elevators and then upended directly into the holds of the waiting colliers. The whole process took a few minutes, and the train of iron tubs would soon be marshalled with the tug again and sent on its way back for another load. Later, with the opening of coal-fired power stations along the route, the Tom Puddings also took on the huge task of keeping them supplied. This inherently simple and efficient system ensured that the Aire & Calder continued to thrive well into the 20th century and remain profitable up to the nationalisation of the waterway network. Improvements were constantly made, such as the enlargement of locks, and the introduction of a new and larger type of compartment boat, designed to carry up to 170 tons. Marshalled in trains of three,

Above: *A pusher tug forces a train of loaded coal barges along the canal near Knottingley, demonstrating that commercial carrying on inland waterways is alive and well in the Northeast, despite the massacre of the coal industry.*

Opposite: *Empty coal barges navigate Castleford Junction, a major waterways crossroads. To the left is the River Aire, going away into the distance is the Wakefield branch, following the course of the River Calder, and to the right and in the foreground is the main line of the Aire & Calder, coming from Leeds.*

Below: *Coal barges loading at the staithe at Mickletown, one of the few still surviving.*

these were designed for the same automated loading and unloading techniques. With the dominance of coal, there was an inevitable reduction of other, more traditional cargoes, and these had mostly disappeared by the end of the 19th century. However, in their place came oil, with the waterway playing an increasingly important role in transporting bulk oil products inland from coastal ports such as Immingham.

The last few years have witnessed, with the virtual extinction of the coal trade in the region, the most significant changes to have occurred in the whole history of the Aire & Calder. The transport of coal does continue, but oil products are now more important in keeping the waterway alive. In many ways the Aire & Calder is a living monument to the former might of the British coal trade, and any exploration of it brings home all too clearly the way the coal industry has been sacrificed to the altar of short-term political expediency. All along the banks

are closed collieries, abandoned and derelict loading staithes and other physical reminders of the days when coal was king. Many a former miner now spends his time fishing the murky waters of the canal that once helped to keep him in business.

Despite this, the Aire & Calder Canal is still a commercial waterway in the proper meaning of the term. It exists for the carriage of cargoes, and earns revenue in the way that it has done since the 18th century. In fact, the large waterways of the Northeast are really the only ones in Britain that are still viable along traditional commercial lines. There are, of course, plenty of pleasure craft using these waters but no pleasure boat in the world can match the vision of a laden barge making its way through an inland landscape. Still common throughout northern and central Europe, this is a rare sight in Britain, and one to be savoured to the full. With its short length of 34 miles from end to end, its relative accessibility, and its range of locks and bridges, docks and quays, and barges and tugs, the Aire & Calder is actually the best place to experience all the excitement of commercial carrying, seen against the background of a landscape that is itself distinctive, and unlike any other in Britain. Here is no theme park or self-conscious heritage centre, merely the raw reality of a way of life that blends history with the demands of modern industry, and produces an exciting result. Only time will tell whether the few surviving commercial waterways of Britain are merely the lingering remnants of a once flourishing network doomed to extinction, or whether by their survival they indicate the way to a more sensible, and environmentally attractive, transport system. Either way they have to be savoured, offering as they do a dramatic contrast to the obvious appeal of the traditional, small scale, rural British canal. I have to admit that I have never seen the Aire & Calder from the deck of a boat, all my explorations having been on foot or by car. I have thus missed the full excitement of a commercial waterway on which large barges have the right of way, and know it, on which the large locks are controlled by traffic

lights and the maritime equivalent of road signs, and on which there are many dramas of a kind inconceivable on conventional canals. Meeting, on a sharp bend, a train of loaded barges being pushed at a solid speed by a powerful tug whose skipper seems unconcerned that he is occupying all the available space on the water, and wishing, as a result, that one's boat was suddenly two feet wide, or better still, not there at all, is something that lingers in the memory, yet it is at the heart of any commercial waterway experience. It is vital to know that real life does exist, and that there is more to canals than colourful boats wandering pointlessly, and in a leisurely fashion, through conventionally delightful countryside.

For all its apparent bleakness, the landscape of the Aire & Calder does have a particular quality. It is, perhaps, a taste far removed from soft hills, quiet woodland, pretty cottages and far-reaching views over gentle fields, but it is certainly one that is worth acquiring. For much of the route the landscape is a low one of long views and huge skies, closer to Holland than Britain. Against the sky are the changing patterns of church spires, silos, and the vast abstract shapes of power station cooling towers. The flatness is a virtue, offering in many places the chance to see that extraordinary vision characteristic of waterways set below a level landscape, a large boat travelling, apparently effortlessly, through a field filled with incurious cows.

The last phase of the building of the Aire & Calder was a broad canal to connect the Aire at Knottingley with the River Ouse. This was completed in 1826, and the direct route it offered soon attracted a great expansion of trade. The place where the canal joined the Ouse was initially a desolate and empty spot, but the canal company began at once to create a network of large enclosed docks, with large ship locks to link them to the river. Large vessels could therefore sail up the Ouse and dock in safety to tranship their cargoes on to the smaller canal boats, or to load with the many

products that British industry was then sending round the world. Once this lock complex was in place, the company then built the necessary infrastructure to support it, including warehouses and offices, housing for the workers, and even a church. Thus the port of Goole came into being, a town, like Stourport on the Staffordshire & Worcestershire Canal, owing its existence entirely to the waterway it served. Created in the bustling 1830s and 1840s, Goole is much larger than Stourport, and it lacks the 18th-century formality of that town. However, it is a town full of interest with a style of its own. At its heart are the docks, a complex range of great expanses of water to the west of the canal. These came first, and so the town has grown up around them. The complete integration of the two creates an atmosphere, and an excitement that cannot really be found in any other canal town in Britain. The first thing about Goole is its skyline, a muddle of cranes, silos,

Opposite: *The open landscape and splendid skies of the Aire & Calder, looking west from Heck Bridge with a distant view of Ferrybridge.*

Below: *All kinds of ships and boats visit Goole docks, with canal tugs and barges much in evidence in the foreground, beneath the town's exciting skyline.*

37

Above: *Coal carriers on the busy run between Kellingley colliery and Ferrybridge power station, with barges loading at the staithe. This is the only place in Britain where the traditional interdependence of the coal industry and canal carrying can still be seen.*

warehouses and the superstructure of ships always held together by the great black spire of St John's Church. All around is dereliction and decay, old abandoned buildings, patches of wasteland, disused coal staithes, battered swing bridges and lines of rusting railway track going nowhere, but the ever-present ships keep it alive. The docks are busy with all kinds of ships, loading and unloading at quays that are still in the very centre of what is still, despite recent attempts at redevelopment, an early 19th-century town. Look at the grandiose, if decayed, hotels and pubs, the grimy but still exuberant public buildings, and the ubiquitous modern shopping centres pale into the insignificance they deserve. The particular quality of Goole is that it is all so accessible. There can be few better places for those who enjoy the excitement of ships and shipping.

As a self-contained harbour town, Goole has no real suburbs, and so the canal passes quickly into the surrounding flat landscape. It runs virtually parallel to the Dutch River, part of the extensive network of waterways dug in the 17th and 18th century in many parts of eastern England to drain the marshlands. It takes its name from Vermuyden, the Dutch engineer responsible for much of this work. The route is then more remote, with little to fill the empty landscape between the banks and the distant horizon of cooling towers and railways embankments. There is a brief view of Cowick Hall, an 18th-century mansion that is now the headquarters of a chemical conglomerate, but this piece of real building looks almost out of place in a setting so unmarked, except for the occasional canalside pub, by conventional architecture. Villages hang back, playing no part, and there is a sense almost of time standing still as a petrol barge creeps along. At a remote cottage, a rough notice offers cooking apples at £1.50 per stone – no metric nonsense in the East Riding. In the middle of nowhere the New Junction Canal branches away to the south, to run straight as a dye for over 5 miles to join the Sheffield & South Yorkshire Navigation. Built in 1905, this offered a direct route to Goole for the coalfields and industrial centres of South Yorkshire. The first lock, large and mechanically controlled, is near Pollington, and then the pattern is broken by the sight of a field full of plastic cruisers, small yachts and other pleasure craft, isolated in the surrounding wilderness. This is Heck Basin, the home of the South Yorkshire Boat Club, an unexpected outburst of canal conventionality. There is another huge lock at Whitley, and then comes Knottingley, a large and traditional industrial town that straddles the waterway. Here the canal from Goole joins the River Aire, still open to boats as the older, and much slower route to the Ouse, which it joins via Haddlesey and the Selby Canal. This navigation dates from the late 18th century, and its success made the old abbey town of Selby into Yorkshire's principal inland port, a position maintained until the development of Goole. Knottingley has mills, chemical works, a huge glass factory making bottles and jars and a river tradition now overshadowed completely by roaring lorries. More appealing are the villages, each a self-contained group of houses, a church and village hall, a farm or two, some pubs and perhaps a few shops, sitting in the middle of nowhere in particular, and full of hidden lives. One such village shop and post office that I went into recently sold only three lines (apart from stamps), confectionery, white socks for schoolgirls, and fishing gear, and it was this that had taken over. Every shelf, every corner, was filled with reels, rods and all other kinds of arcane equipment designed to tempt muddy and tasteless fish from the bottom of dirty canals. There were new and secondhand items, and even the latter were of staggering cost. It seems to take hundreds of pounds to become fully prepared for the great adventure of battling with the creatures that lead their gloomy lives in rivers and canals. I know that fishing is by far and away the most popular sport in Britain, but I have never understood why escaping the wife and children and sitting all day by a canal, eating crisps and chocolate bars, and waiting for some fish to attach

Right: *A canalside garden at Knottingley.*

Below: *Colourful narrow boats leaving the flood lock at Ferrybridge. They will pass under the concrete A1 viaduct and then turn left into the canal. To the right is the River Aire, with the stone arches of the old 18th-century bridge that used to carry the Great North Road.*

itself to the dangling hook, is called sport. And why are fishermen, and 99 per cent of the time it is men, so dour, gloomy, uncommunicative and often quite hostile when they are spending their time doing something they presumably have chosen to do? I have spent untold hours on canals, either on boats, or walking the towpath, and I can remember only one occasion when a fisherman spoke to me, of his own free will, and in a friendly fashion. He showed me all his equipment, explained what you did with a ledgering pole, and told me what it all cost, and I was even more staggered then. The village post office with its packed shelves merely brought it all back again. This mysterious activity, apparently called coarse fishing, seems entirely well-named. To an outsider it seems infinitely boring, often cold and miserable, wildly expensive, and ultimately pointless as the wretched things that get caught are uneatable and get thrown back into the water, probably mutilated in the process. But I suppose anything is better than having to spend time with the family.

Fishermen also seem to be in a permanent state of undeclared war with other canal users, based on a deep unwillingness to share whatever the canal has to offer. Anyone on a boat, approaching a long line of fishermen hunched over their gear, will know that they are in for a series of blank stares, enraged looks, grunts and bits of muttered abuse. I used to

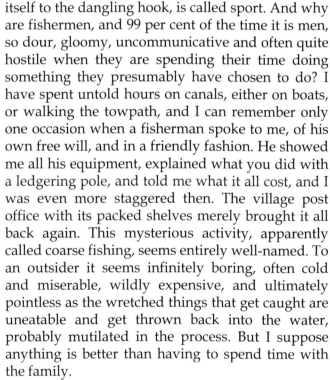

try to forestall this by grinning cheerily, waving and showing by other well-tried means that I was friendly, and delighted that they were also enjoying the canal, but it was always a complete waste of time. The next stage was to be aggressive and ask questions that required an answer. I soon gave up simple inanities like 'Are they biting well today?', because I quickly learned that one of the main pleasures derived from coarse fishing seems to be getting cross because there is nothing to catch.

More direct attacks, along the lines of why didn't they want to share the canal, generally produced an even more sullen silence, so I gave that up as well. I'm afraid I soon reached the next stage, which is to stare resolutely at the opposite bank until the fishermen are well past. Boats stir up the water, spread mud and weeds, and probably scatter the fish, so I can see how the resentment arises. Impossible to understand, however, is similar resentment directed towards walkers and towpath cyclists. Fishermen always have so much gear for an activity that seems to demand little more than a piece of string and a bent pin, and they often spread it all over the towpath, forcing passers-by to step gingerly between pieces of expensive machinery, cartons of squirming maggots, thermos flasks, and an astonishing variety of very long rods. God help you if you so much as touch anything. And God help you even more if you are even tempted to try a spot of fishing yourself, for you will soon learn that the fishing rights over virtually every inch of even the most obscure British canal are held by private angling clubs apparently located many miles from the stretch in question. There can be no sight more terrible than a fully enraged fisherman defending his rightful territory.

Knottingley is one of the places where boats are controlled by traffic lights, and mechanisation is certainly a feature of the next few miles. The scene is completely dominated by the huge power stations at Ferrybridge, in their own way powerfully impressive and exciting. As an unexpected contrast, at the heart of it all, is the

18th-century, three-arched bridge that formerly served the old Great North Road, with its matching toll house. It is just possible to imagine the mail coaches clattering over the bridge, distant ghosts beneath its huge concrete replacement. Between here and Leeds, industry is the key. Coal, the deposed king, is still powerful here even in retirement, and continues to shape the landscape. Most pits have been swept away, but their marks are ineradicable. Vast excavators drag the coal from open cast sites, and trains of loaded coal barges are still to be seen. Castleford is a centre of real commercial boating, with a variety of tugs, barges and other craft to be seen, particularly around the locks, and the busy waterways crossroads formed by the Aire & Calder, the Wakefield branch which follows the navigable route of the Calder, and the old course of the Aire, winding its unnavigable way through the town.

The Calder to Wakefield, navigable at least since the late 17th century, and regularly enlarged and modernised ever since, is now virtually a canal. Its straight route cuts out all the natural wanderings of

Above: *The lock keeper at the controls of the fully mechanised Bulholme lock, with the old raising bridge in the background.*

Opposite: *A narrow boat east of Bulholme lock, dwarfed by the elegant arch of the old railway bridge.*

Above: *With its extravagant Doric columns and fine iron arch, the original Stanley Ferry aqueduct is a monument to the canal age. Opened in 1839, it is supposed to have inspired Sydney Harbour Bridge. Its modern concrete replacement is alongside.*

the river, but it is never far away. At Stanley Ferry a huge iron aqueduct crosses the river. This splendidly tough but elegant piece of engineering, opened in 1839, should be seen both from the minor road below, and close-to from the towpath. Apparently its striking design, with the waterway carried in an iron trough by a great iron arch, was the inspiration for Sydney Harbour Bridge, built a century later. It still stands but traffic now goes over a modern replacement. The canal offers good views as it approaches Wakefield, before making its way through the city centre to join the Calder & Hebble Navigation after the curiously named Fall Ing lock. This runs for 21 miles to Sowerby Bridge, the

present end of the line. However, it was not always thus, for the Calder & Hebble used, in its heyday, to connect with two out of the three trans-Pennine waterways. First was the junction with the Huddersfield canals, whose dramatic route across the mountains had at its centre the famous Standedge tunnel, at 5,456yds by far the longest in Britain, and then at Sowerby Bridge the Rochdale Canal began its steep climb towards Manchester on the other side. Although long closed, and in some places actually filled in, both the Rochdale and the Huddersfield Narrow canals are subject to ambitious restoration projects. At present, the only way across the Pennines by boat is via the Leeds &

Liverpool Canal, but one day it may be possible to explore by boat the extraordinary engineering skills that brought the other two into existence. At the moment they are both magnificent long-distance towpath walks, and every boater's dream of travelling through Standedge tunnel is still tantalisingly just out of reach.

The past is around on all canals, but infinitely more so on those that run through centres of industry. On a wandering rural route it is always possible to imagine the gentle clopping of the towing horse and the silent glide of the boat through the water, but somehow it is industry that really fires the imagination. By its nature it is forever changing, but leaving behind tangible remains filled with ghosts of the past. The recent past of the Aire & Calder Canal, and its associated waterways, is coal, but the remains of this devastated industry are still so visible that, without any of the softening stamp of history and nature that will one day be laid over them, the response they provoke is one of despair. The real ghosts of Castleford and Ferrybridge are the potters of the late 18th and early 19th centuries, skilful men and women who made great quantities of delicate creamware and fine white stoneware, before vanishing without a trace, their only legacy today being the beautiful pots they created, handsome domestic wares now fought over by collectors and mummified in display cases.

The approach to Leeds is entirely industrial, but hills now break up the dominant flatness of the landscape and add a welcome change to the views. The canal drops down through a series of dramatic locks and then in the very heart of the city the Aire & Calder ends where it meets the Leeds & Liverpool. For years this was a setting of romantic and rather sinister gloom, dark stone warehouses lowering presences over the locks and the murky waters of the basin. Today, city centre regeneration is turning it into something bright and cheerful. What such changes do to the essential spirit of the canal is a matter of debate.

Above: *Crown Point bridge, and architecture old and new flanking the canal in the heart of Leeds.*

PLACES TO VISIT

Bradford: National Museum of Photography, Film and Television, the past, present and future of the media excitingly displayed; IMAX screen.
Colour Museum, run by the Society of Dyers and Colourists, shows optical illusions, the effects of light and colour, and the story of dyeing and textile printing.
Harewood House and Bird Garden, 8 miles N of Leeds centre: 18th-century stately home with 'Capability' Brown grounds; aviaries, adventure playground, etc.
Leeds: Armley Mills Museum, Armley, once the world's largest woollen mill, working now to tell

story of wool from sheep to knitwear.
Kirkstall Abbey, well-preserved Cistercian abbey of 12th-century foundation, on the banks of the River Aire; folk museum with Victorian shops, workshops and cottages.
Middleton Colliery Railway, Moor Road Station, steam trains run at weekends in season along this, the first railway authorised by an Act of Parliament (in 1758).
Thwaite Mills, Stourton, 2 miles S of city centre: stone for putty and paint was crushed at this restored mill between the River Aire and the Aire & Calder; a display in the Georgian mill-owner's house tells the story.

Nostell Priory, 4 miles SE of Wakefield: a Palladian house built 1733, with additional wing and many state rooms by Adam; notable collection of Chippendale furniture, made for the house (National Trust); lakeside walks.
Pontefract Castle: remains of the 13th–14th-century great tower and some walls.
Snaith: large priory church of Norman origins.
Stanley Ferry: Ferry Boat, popular canalside pub in converted warehouse with view of aqueduct, river and marina.
Wakefield: Art Gallery has rooms devoted to local sculptors Barbara Hepworth and Henry Moore.

The Kennet and Avon Canal

THE KENNET & AVON can claim to be the grandest canal in Britain, and the journey westwards from London to Bath and Bristol is certainly one of the great waterway experiences. Cutting right across southern England, this broad canal is a magnificent exploration of the changing nature of the landscape along a route made memorable by the quality of the architecture and the scale of the engineering. It is also one of the notable achievements of Neo-Classicism and the late 18th-century spirit of enlightenment and rationalism.

There is, of course, an age-old tradition of great journeys between London and Bristol. Good communications between the capital and the major English seaport had long been seen as essential and there was by the latter part of the 18th century an efficient network of turnpikes and toll roads that supported regular and quick stage coach services. The Great West Road is certainly not a creation of the motor car. The importance of the journey was further underlined by the social and architectural development of Bath in the late 18th century, a period when that city rediscovered the status it had enjoyed in Roman times. As a result, passenger transport between London, Bath and Bristol was, in the context of its time, excellent. Freight was another matter altogether, and throughout the 18th century it was quicker for freight traffic to be carried in sailing vessels all round the southern coast of England than dragged along the roads in the lumbering and painfully slow goods wagons of the day.

Approaching Bath along the Avon Valley, the canal, railway and river run side by side, framed by a distant line of hills.

The Kennet and Avon Canal

From the junction of the River Kennet and the River Thames near Reading to Hanham Lock, the start of the tidal River Avon, near Bristol 86 ½ miles long, with 105 broad locks

Notable features River Kennet and locks at Reading, River Kennet and locks at Newbury, the canal west of Hungerford town, views over the Vale of Pewsey, Crofton locks and steam pumping engines, Bruce tunnel, Caen Hill flight of locks near Devizes, remains of Wiltshire & Berkshire Canal, Bradford on Avon wharf, Avoncliff aqueduct, Dundas aqueduct, Claverton water pump, in Bath the canal route and bridges, the views of the city, the Widcombe flight of locks and the River Avon, from Hanham the tidal River Avon, Bristol harbour and docks.

History The Kennet and Avon is one of the greatest of Britain's long-distance waterways, its architecture and engineering a spectacular answer to the landscape through which it passes. It was built to allow large barges to travel direct from London to Bristol. There are three distinct sections, first the Kennet Navigation from its junction with the River Thames at Reading to Newbury, opened in 1723, and second the Avon Navigation from Bath to Hanham and Bristol, opened four years later. The third section, linking these two river navigations, is a 57-mile canal, with 79 broad locks, designed by the engineer John Rennie. Construction started in 1794, but the work was not completed until 1810, having been plagued by financial shortages and engineering difficulties. Despite its obvious potential as a major cross-country route, the Kennet and Avon never fulfilled its promise. Coal was the major cargo, mostly from the Somerset coalfields, along with agricultural produce, but the canal was never able to compete seriously with the established coastal trading routes. Its late completion date and continuing problems of water supply further limited its success and, within 30 years of its opening, the Great Western Railway was able to transport freight from London to Bristol in under three hours. The canal owners, who by then operated the whole route, having bought out the two river navigations, struggled on for a while, but in 1852 they gave in and sold the whole enterprise to the Great Western Railway. From then on, with declining traffic and reduced standards of maintenance, the pattern was one of steady but gradual decay. Commercial traffic, by then entirely localised, died out completely in the 1930s, and by the late 1940s much of the canal was impassable. It was closed in the early 1950s. By then, however, a canal association had been formed to campaign for full reopening. This led to the launching of the Kennet and Avon Canal Trust in 1962, and the start of a massive restoration programme, based largely on voluntary labour. Section by section the whole canal was brought back to life, its bed dredged and re-lined, the locks and structures repaired, and after about 30 years of toil the whole route was reopened to boats. The restoration of the Kennet and Avon marked a turning point in public attitudes towards waterways as a whole.

Below: *Two narrow boats prepare to descend the Caen Hill lock flight near Devizes.*

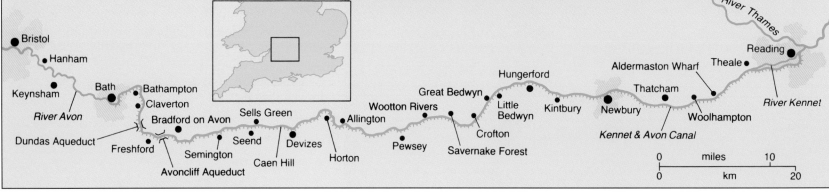

It was the need to improve the transport of freight that inspired the creation of the Kennet & Avon. The full journey from London to Bristol is made up of four parts. The first is the Thames, a major artery at least since the Roman period, and a fully fledged navigation by the 18th century. At Reading the Thames is joined by the Kennet, and this river had been made navigable as far as Newbury by 1723. At the far end is the Avon, which was in use as a navigation from Bath to Bristol by 1727. The fourth section, from Newbury to Bath, is the canal.

It was this that caused the problems. Various schemes were considered through the latter part of the 18th century, but it was not until 1794 that the canal received its parliamentary authorisation. Bearing in mind the importance of the route, and the obvious appeal to investors of a waterway linking London and Bristol, this late date is extraordinary. By this time, canals had been a feature of British life for over 30 years and much of the national network was either in use or under construction. There seemed to be no problem in raising money for the most hare-brained of schemes, yet the Kennet & Avon was always short of supporters, financial and otherwise. The route was certainly difficult and expensive to build, but such considerations were no deterrent in other parts of the country. In any case, complex engineering problems and high costs had been faced and overcome by John Hore, the builder of both the Kennet and the Avon navigations. The short journey between Reading and Newbury had required the building of 18 broad locks in as many miles, and over ten miles of completely new waterway, while on the Avon his problems were quite different, a dramatic tidal fall and a fast-flowing river making its way through hilly countryside. The pressure to bridge the 57-mile gap between these two successful river navigations must have been considerable, and yet the Kennet & Avon Canal was not finally completed until 1810. By that time it was almost too late, and its potential

as a major cross-country waterway was certainly never realised. The bulk of the freight traffic continued to be sailed round the south coast and by the 1830s steam ships were offering significant reductions in the journey time. Even more important was the challenge posed by the railway. Less than 30 years after the canal was opened, Brunel's Great Western Railway could carry passengers and freight between London and Bristol in under three hours. The canal never really recovered and its owners gave up the struggle in 1852 and sold out to the railway company. For the

Above: *Colourful narrow boats moored in Hungerford basin. The bridge in the background carries the town's main street.*

Above: *A narrow boat in the dry dock at Bradford on Avon wharf receives a new coat of paint.*

Opposite: *A London-bound Intercity 125 hurtles past Little Bedwyn, while a narrow boat makes a more leisurely journey westwards as a crew member winds the paddle to fill the lock.*

next century it quietly declined, relying for its income on essentially local traffic. Even this had ceased by the late 1930s and by the 1940s the canal was virtually impassable, the route shallow and overgrown, the locks leaking or collapsed, the bridges and structures uncared for. In the early 1950s it was closed.

I first became aware of the Kennet & Avon in the early 1960s. At that time I had a girlfriend who lived near Chippenham, and many long hours were spent travelling up and down the Great West Road on my elderly and extremely slow Francis Barnett motorcycle. Sometimes I would break the journeys by leaving the main road and taking one of the many lanes that led quickly to bridges, first over Brunel's railway and then over the canal. For long stretches these three transport systems lay side by side, each engineer in his turn realising that his predecessor had chosen the best route. There were a number of places where I could rest my machine, unbend my rigid limbs and watch the lovely green-painted Great Western locomotives, the Castles, and Halls, and occasionally the huge Kings, go thundering past. At the same time I could look out over the derelict canal, picturesque in its natural decay, and wonder about its history. After a while the Chippenham house was sold, the girl moved on to other things and the canal went out of my mind. My next visit was several years later, and by this time I knew quite a bit about its history, vital background needed for writing about the canal in a waterway guide. Not long before, a small publisher had, out of the blue, asked me to write a book about the Thames and had suggested that the best way to get to know the river was to walk its length. This I duly did. I spread the walking over a long wet winter, and had a wonderful time, sometimes marching along on my own, sometimes with friends who were persuaded to spend a day or so sharing this madness. As ever, the schedule was impossible, the problems unpredictable and endless, and the writing fitted somehow into evenings and weekends, but it all eventually came

together and the book appeared. The publisher moved on to other waterways, and to a series of books about canals in Britain. I should have realised then that writing was not all it was cracked up to be, but I was seduced by the enjoyment of the research and the excitement of doing it all under pressure. I was also young, and needed a job. The Kennet & Avon came up in Book Three, and by that time my waterways knowledge and experience had greatly increased. I had explored many canals, by boat, on foot and by car. The Kennet & Avon, then still largely derelict, was at first sight a natural candidate for a car survey, a quick but thorough study of its highlights, as befitted an unnavigable waterway in a book about navigable rivers and canals. In the event we decided that this approach would be unsatisfactory for so important a waterway, and so I dusted off my walking boots again. Over the next few weeks I walked from Reading to Bristol, a journey of about 90 miles, broken up into sections of ten or 20 miles. A day or so of walking would be followed by a few days in the office, writing up what I had seen. It was a most memorable walk, a journey across England at a pace that made sense of the complex patterns of history, landscape and architecture through which the canal passes.

For historical reasons, it seemed essential to follow the route westwards and so we started at Reading. I say 'we' because the Kennet & Avon walk was shared with a girlfriend who had been convinced, somewhat against her natural inclinations, that the experience would be enjoyable. She had known me during my Thames walking days, and so was not entirely ignorant of what lay ahead. In the event we had a good time, although there were one or two rather forceful exchanges of views, notably while standing in pouring rain on a soggy towpath that seemed to stretch interminably into an empty landscape. We started by taking a train to Reading, a mundane activity made memorable by our having the full British Rail breakfast, with all its trimmings, in the

half hour that the train took from Paddington, thanks to a helpful steward who clearly enjoyed the challenge.

Trains featured strongly in the first few days of the walk, because they are never very far from the canal. Waterway and railway run virtually side by side from Reading nearly all the way to Pewsey, and quiet moments in the remote landscape were regularly shattered by expresses howling down the Great Western towards Exeter and all points west. And in those days they did howl, for still in service were those distinctive maroon-coloured diesel locomotives known as Westerns, all with names like *Western Fusilier* and *Western Ranger,* and only to be found in this part of Britain. Nothing could replace the Castles and Kings, but at least they seemed to carry an echo of the GWR pedigree.

A close relationship between canal and railway can be found all over England, a reflection of the remarkable surveying skills of those 18th-century engineers. With little more than a horse and some basic equipment they ranged all over the country, seeking out the best routes. It is extraordinary how often they got it right. The next generation of engineers, planning the railway network, often followed closely in their footsteps, and in this century the motorway builders have done the same. The M1 never ventures far from the Grand Union Canal all the way from North London to well beyond Rugby. The engineer for the Kennet & Avon was John Rennie, a man able to marry fine architecture and engineering skills in a way that set him apart from so many of his peers. In the canal age, only Thomas Telford could do the same. Most of the other canal builders could handle the basic engineering, and were good surveyors, but their architecture was generally as rudimentary as their cost accounting. The canals of England are surrounded by pleasant, workmanlike structures that sit well in their landscape, but rarely excite. By comparison, the great railway engineers were architects of consummate skill. The simplest building designed by Brunel has style and grace,

while his grand structures laid down new standards of architectural excellence. Rennie was, therefore, a remarkable man and he set out to build a canal whose architecture was memorable. This was to be one of the reasons why it took so long to build the Kennet & Avon. The engineer was simply spending too much of the shareholders' money building fine-looking bridges from well-cut stone, and not paying enough attention to the canal's practical necessities. It has to be said that in some of its engineering the Kennet & Avon was not a great success. Rennie made the serious error of designing a canal with a short summit level and so there was never enough water to feed the locks at either end. It had been well known for years that a canal could operate efficiently only if it had a long summit level, continuously fed from reservoirs and from rivers and streams. As a result, pumps had to be installed to maintain the water supply and during periods of dry weather the canal often came to a halt. Other sections were built over porous rock and leaked continuously, further reducing the supplies of water and necessitating yet more pumping. Nevertheless, the Kennet & Avon was a great achievement. The 57-mile route from Newbury to Bath has no less than 79 broad locks that take it up to its summit at Savernake, 474ft above sea level, and down again. Each of those locks used 50,000 gallons of water every time a boat passed through, water that had to be quickly replaced if the canal was to operate smoothly. Thus, it could take as much as 3 million gallons to transport a boat the whole length of the waterway from Reading to Bristol. Rennie's errors must have played a part in the Kennet & Avon's failure to live up to expectations.

The difference between the Kennet & Avon when I walked it from end to end, and the Kennet & Avon now, is, of course, radical. I explored a romantic ghost, the lingering legacy of a great waterway, whereas now it is a fully working canal. Its restoration is one of the great triumphs of post-war Britain, and the successful completion of

Opposite: *Near All Cannings the canal crosses a remote corner of Wiltshire, with Baston Hill and Horton Down in the background.*

Above: *The eastern portal of Bruce tunnel, surrounded by the dense greenery of late summer.*

the project in 1990 is a unique achievement never likely to be matched. Crossing as it does the shire heartlands of southern England, and at no point having been an industrial waterway, the Kennet & Avon was never short of friends, and restoration plans were being prepared in the early 1950s. At a time of large scale closures and a general lack of interest in the whole area of canals and waterways, there were a few enthusiasts who felt that the Kennet & Avon represented the last line of defence. Here they chose to stand and fight, knowing that the outcome of the battle would probably determine the future of Britain's waterways network. It was an immensely ambitious task, the full restoration of one of Britain's largest and most complex canals. In 1962 the Kennet & Avon Canal Trust was formed to fight for restoration, and to bring these impossible dreams towards reality. In the end, the dream did become reality, but the 30 years it took was nearly double the time taken to build the canal in the first place. Work started at the eastern end, gradually extending the Kennet Navigation westwards to Newbury, and then onwards towards Hungerford. At the same time, the long labour of repairing the various lock flights along the route began. The work was carried out

largely by volunteers, small groups at first, later swelled by working parties of boy scouts, soldiers, and even prisoners. The British Waterways Board, at first wholly uninterested, came bit by bit to support the project totally, and it was this practical support that turned restoration from a wild dream into something attainable. Funds were raised from all kinds of sources, and year by year the navigable sections of canal inched forwards. The detached pieces in the middle joined up, and spread slowly but surely towards the sections at each end. The large scale engineering tasks, generally beyond the level of volunteer abilities, were taken on by professional companies, and by this means the Bath flight was rebuilt, the pumping stations were brought back into use and the leaking sections given new concrete linings. Left to the end were the real challenges, the huge Devizes flight of locks, and the places where new crossings were required where canal and main road met. And when these were the only remaining barriers to complete restoration, ways were found to overcome the difficulties they posed. The successful completion of the project is an astonishing achievement, and boats can now once more make their way from London to Bristol.

That, of course, is not the end of the story. The canal continues to have its problems, with water supply being at the head of the list. Many of the things that must have kept Rennie awake at night are still there, now plaguing a new generation of engineers. Above all else, the Kennet & Avon has made it clear that reopening a canal is only half the battle. Keeping it open and working well is ultimately a far more demanding challenge, for there can be no end to it. No one wants to see ever again a repeat of the saga of the Stratford-on-Avon Canal, a waterway similarly restored by volunteers and reopened amid great rejoicing in 1964, only to be virtually impassable again within ten years through lack of maintenance.

The Kennet leaves the Thames not far from Reading Station, and so our walk was quickly

1960s. I had done my share of marching in those days of idealism, and so it was curious to see it again in a very different, and more natural context. The Aldermaston marches were a feature of the Easter weekend, as was a very different Kennet & Avon activity, the annual Devizes to Westminster canoe race. The canal formed a major part of its route but its condition in those days necessitated a considerable amount of portaging. I watched it once, and the sight of men, and women, struggling for miles along muddy paths with their canoes in their arms made me absolutely certain that it was high on the list of things I never wanted to do. I think we called a halt at Thatcham, and spent the night in an hotel there, reaching Newbury the next day, where the canal was once again navigable for a few miles. It was a quiet walk through a landscape of water meadows fringed by distant hills and woods, with the occasional glimpse of a church spire or the grand facade of someone's country house. Little has changed today and Newbury is still a good riverside town, with the canal cutting its way through the centre. It is one of those places where, locked in the private world of the canal boat, you look up at a bridge and are amazed at the sight of buses, women shopping with pushchairs and people generally going about their business, the head-on clash of two very different worlds.

under way, although interrupted for a while by the lack of towpath. Nowadays riverside Reading is quite attractive, probably the best face of a town whose excellent Victorian heart has been ripped apart by the meretricious modernism of England's silicon valley. There are a couple of locks and then the suburbs give way to more open countryside. As we walked on, with the landscape steadily improving, it looked as though I might get away with my rash promises about the pleasures to be drawn from the experience. Locks and the occasional swing bridge added interest, and small villages supplied our basic needs. In those days, Tyle Mill near Sulhamstead was the limit of navigation. From this point it was very much a case of into the unknown. The railway was ever present, running straight alongside the waterway's meanderings as the navigation moved constantly in and out of the course of the Kennet. We passed Aldermaston, a place known not so much for its pretty village as for its fame as the starting point for the great annual CND protest marches of the early

Above: *The Kennet Navigation in the modern heart of Reading with, in the foreground, a visitor from Warwickshire, underlining the national appeal of the reopened canal.*

Right: *Careful brickwork on the restored lock at Woolhampton. The raised bricks give leverage for the feet when opening the heavy lock gates, a traditional idea brought up to date.*

Opposite: A hot afternoon at Crofton lock, with spectators enjoying a canalside picnic while the old steam pump pours black smoke into the summer sky.

Below: *Stoking the boiler for the great steam pumps at Crofton.*

There having been no disasters or disputes, my friend agreed to come on the next section too, and we duly set off from Newbury into a lovely stretch of canal, then recently restored, that ran through woods and rolling hills. The Kennet, now just a river again, flowed beside the canal, its route masked by a series of watermills. Fast-flowing, and a noted trout stream, the Kennet added greatly to the setting. The villages were uniformly quiet and pretty, but Avington's little Norman church was, and is, well worth a detour. And so we came to Hungerford, then a lively market town whose steep and handsome main street was still full of real shops. Now, it is a different place, having sold out almost wholly to the antique trade; fine if you like that kind of thing, but not much good if you are after a good joint of lamb, a pound of russets or some fish fingers.

West of Hungerford there is a wonderful stretch, the canal set high above the river and its water meadows, looking down to the church. All this was then derelict, and overgrown, and all around the cattle browsed quietly among the buttercups. It was

a rural sight out of some 18th-century landscape painting, and all that was missing was the squire on his horse, admiring his acres, while his wife sat taking tea with the children.

From here on the scenery became more exciting, distant views broken by hills and pockets of woodland, the steady sequence of broken locks separating the stretches of reed-filled ditch that the canal had become. Along this stretch, and indeed all along the Kennet & Avon, are old pillboxes and great concrete tank traps mouldering in the bushes. Years ago I thought this was the remains of some Dad's Army panic about the Germans invading by canal boat. Now older, and wiser, I realise that the canal, cutting across the country, probably represented a major line of last defence in 1940. I liked the idea of the Germans arriving dressed, not as nuns, but as bargees. Little Bedwyn was then, and still is, a lovely village, a fine church and a row of decorative early Victorian Gothic cottages facing the canal, a lock, and then the grander houses on the southern slope of the valley. Also good is Great Bedwyn's church, with its powerful crossing tower and pretty graveyard. A visit to the village's stone museum is essential, still a remarkable pocket of English eccentricity.

We pressed on, the Crofton locks coming thick and fast as we approached the canal's summit. The only trouble was that it was now raining hard and seemed set for the day. It was, without doubt, what my grandmother used to call wet rain, and we were soon very damp indeed. The tall chimney of Crofton pumping station loomed out of the mist, and I barely gave it a glance. Many years were to pass before I finally saw its great 1812 Boulton and Watt steam pump in action. This massively sedate and elegant machine is the oldest working beam engine in the world, and watching it doing its stuff is simply unforgettable, a vision from the past akin to seeing prehistoric monsters grazing by some primeval swamp. We reached the top lock and walked on to the short Bruce tunnel. My friend had been making it very clear for some time that she

Above: *Old canal cottages and the preserved crane at Burbage wharf.*

was not enjoying herself, and now said that she was going home, this minute. In despair, for I knew from experience that such pronouncements were to be taken seriously, I looked at the map. All around us lay the wild emptiness of the Savernake Forest, and not much else. In the pre-Beeching era Savernake boasted, for obscure railway reasons, two stations, but these had long disappeared, and the trains roaring past were definitely non-stop. We walked, not speaking, up the steep bank by the tunnel mouth, making for a minor road that crossed above the tunnel. I suppose I had some vain hope of stopping a tractor, or a district nurse on her rounds. By then, I would have flung myself on my knees in front of anything passing, even the vicar on his bicycle, to try to redeem a situation already seriously out of control. When we reached the road, there, in the middle of nowhere, and sent down by some merciful god, was a small hotel. We booked ourselves in, got rid of the soggy clothes, and over a

lunch of local trout, friendly relations were re-established. I have passed that hotel many times since then, but never without a little nod of thanks.

The next day was sunny, and we walked on through the undulating landscape and into an increasingly remote region. Near Pewsey the railway turns away to the south, and then all is quiet, the canal alternating between cutting and embankment, with fine views out over the Vale of Pewsey. Little village wharves, some still complete with crane, hint at the agricultural nature of the cargoes during the long period of decline, but the canal then was little more than a shadow of history across empty fields. Fine churches mark the quiet villages, Alton Priors, All Cannings, Bishop's Cannings, names that carry the clear stamp of essential Englishness.

We spent a night in Devizes, a town almost bypassed by the canal but close to one of the great waterway wonders of Britain, the Caen Hill flight of

29 broad locks that drop the canal dramatically down into the Wiltshire Plain. Then, with broken lock gates and empty pounds, all overgrown, and even grazed by horses and goats, it seemed unreal, remote, some primitive pre-Columbian structure whose significance was lost in history. The idea of those locks once again carrying boats up and down the hill seemed pure fantasy, and yet it has all come to be, thanks to the dedication of the Kennet & Avon's patient restorers.

Away from the locks, the canal leaves behind the hills and crosses an empty countryside. At Semington there once was a junction with the Wiltshire & Berkshire Canal, a somewhat unlikely waterway that wound its way along a tortuous and rather indirect route from here to the Thames near Abingdon. Opened in 1810, it was one of those canals that never did much, its limited traffic eventually stopping for good in 1906. It was closed soon after and little of its 45-mile route remains to be seen. Even more obscure was a branch from this to the Thames & Severn Canal at Latton. This was

Below: *The restored Caen Hill flight near Devizes, a daunting sight for any crew members detailed to work the boat up the locks.*

Right: *A narrow boat travels eastwards along a quiet stretch of canal near Hilperton Marsh.*

Below: *A British Waterways employee 'racking up' at a lock gate on the Caen Hill flight.*

known as the North Wiltshire Canal, but all has vanished into the mists of time and distant memory, all the hopes of the promoters and the shareholders reduced to a fragmentary dotted line on an Ordnance Survey map. During my Thames walk I had visited Latton, and stood in the centre of what had been a thriving canal basin. It was then a barely perceptible depression in a large grassy field, unrecognisable to anyone who did not know what they were looking at, and offering nothing that could bring back all those lives that had been dependent upon it.

From here the Kennet & Avon moves gradually into the narrowing valley of the River Avon. River and canal slowly come together, shortly after two aqueducts carry the canal over, firstly, the railway and secondly a smaller river, the Biss. Going over the top of a train in a boat is a rather bizarre sensation, but it is actually the second aqueduct that draws the eye, its handsome classical arch paving the way for the architectural splendours that lie

ahead. Bradford on Avon is a fine stone town, spread over the steep valley sides, and full of treats, from a Saxon church to Victorian Gothic factories and all in between, but the canal stays high above it. Walking down into the town from the attractive wharf is most enjoyable. Beyond Bradford the Avon and the canal run close together, through the dramatic wooded valley. Everything from now on is drama and magnificence, and Rennie's architectural legacy is a series of theatrical presentations that build up to the climax of Bath. First is the grand Avoncliff aqueduct, stone-built and firmly classical, which carries the canal across the valley. When we walked along this stretch, the canal was dry and overgrown, its course hidden among the trees, and the battered and patched aqueduct looked like some picturesque Piranesi ruin. Restoration has removed some of this romantic appeal, but it is still splendid. Next comes the Dundas aqueduct, a magnificent three-arched stone structure that strides across the valley. It has to be seen from below, by the river, or better still from a distance, in order to enjoy to the full Rennie's command of architecture and the way this great bridge actually improves the natural amphitheatre of the valley. The canal and all its works have to be seen as components in a grand 18th-century classical park, an ideal landscape in which man has demonstrated his control over the forces of nature.

Beside the aqueduct there is a wharf, then quietly decaying, now housing a boatyard. This marks the spot where the Somersetshire Coal Canal met the Kennet & Avon. Opened in 1805, this supplied the canal's primary *raison d'être*, the carriage of coal away from Somerset to the towns that lay along the route to London. The Coal Canal was an extraordinary waterway, built to serve the 30-plus pits then active in the Somerset field, and constructed across a hilly landscape that seemed to present impenetrable barriers to canal builders. Rennie surveyed the original route, and the hills were conquered by tramways, inclined planes and flights of locks. This canal also witnessed the only

Right: *The Dundas aqueduct over the River Avon, a fine example of Rennie's elegant classical architecture.*

Below: *A peaceful mooring for narrow boats and an elegant skiff near Bradford on Avon.*

full scale trial of Robert Weldon's extraordinary caisson lock. In this a loaded boat was floated into a huge wooden box, and then sealed in, presumably with its hapless crew. The box was then lowered 88ft down a brick-lined vertical shaft of massive dimensions, at which point the box was opened and the boat sailed forth on to a lower canal. Luckily, this nightmarish contraption never worked and was quickly abandoned, but its great shaft and box, perhaps still holding some ancient boat, may cause wonder and amazement to archaeologists exploring the ruins of our civilisation some few centuries hence. The Coal Canal was active through the 19th century but was ultimately eclipsed by railways, to be finally closed in 1904. Its route survives in places, a faint echo of a once great industry that has gone, almost without a trace. How many people today, walking their dogs over the steep hills of north Somerset, realise that some of those wooded hills are actually the old waste tips from the Somerset coalfield?

From Dundas the valley opens, and canal, river and railway make their way together through a widening landscape towards Bath. Grand houses mark the route, first Claverton Manor, home of the American Museum, and then Warleigh Manor. Claverton is also the site of the water-driven pump installed in 1813 to lift water 53ft from the Avon to the canal. It was designed by Rennie, one of a number of inventive, but desperate solutions to the problems caused by water shortage.

The approach to Bath is a grand climax, the final tableau in a presentation whose excitement is not matched by any other canal in England. From its vantage point high on the hillside, the canal enters the city in triumph, its route offering unsurpassed views over the city and its architecture. Fine houses line its banks, and then it sweeps in a cutting through Sydney Gardens and into a short tunnel

Right: *The canal's approach to Bath offers an excellent view of the city.*

with a grand classical portico. Bridges are either stone or decorative cast iron. A second tunnel carries elegant 18th-century houses actually over the canal, and then, as the cutting ends, the Kennet & Avon comes to its grand finale, high above the city, at the top of the flight of locks that carry it down to join the River Avon.

It has to be said that after so much architectural splendour, the River Avon comes as rather an anti-climax. We walked through Bath's industrial fringes, seeking the Avon's towpath among old factories populated by ravenous Alsatians. Gradually, and in its own time, the river makes its way through all this muddle and mess towards open countryside, its winding route interrupted from time to time by large locks and their accompanying weirs. The Avon Valley is wide and gentle, the river flanked by broad fields. It was in such a field that we attracted the attention of a herd of cows. Inquisitive beasts that they are, they left their peaceful chewing and rushed towards us, forming a tight circle that pushed us slowly but inexorably towards the river. The more we shouted and flapped our maps, the more they drove us towards the water. They looked amiable enough,

but behind those big brown eyes there was clearly some mischievous intent. What started as farce promised to turn into a scene from some yet-to-be-made Hitchcock drama called *The Cows*. And then, at the moment when a plunge into the Avon seemed the only escape, they all suddenly lost interest and wandered away again.

We pressed on, following the big river's flowing curves past Keynsham, stamped for ever with the lugubrious tones and rash promises of Horace Batchelor of Radio Luxembourg fame, past a chocolate factory whose heavy, sweet smell filled the landscape, past Hanham lock, the start of the tidal Avon, and through a steeply wooded valley to Bristol. With a sense of triumph we made our way to the city centre, and then to Temple Meads Station. Later, sweeping along Brunel's beautifully engineered railway, we watched the canal from the window. In under two hours we covered a journey that had taken us days of walking. It was no wonder the Kennet & Avon could not compete with the Great Western Railway. It was then, and still is, a magnificent canal, but it is also in many respects a magnificent failure. And therein lies its appeal, as perhaps the greatest 18th-century folly of them all.

Above: *Sydney Gardens and Cleveland House mark the canal's triumphant entry into Bath.*

PLACES TO VISIT

The American Museum, Claverton Manor, 2 miles SE of Bath: a collection of American decorative arts, displayed in period furnished rooms; sections on Shakers and on the American Indians, and a beautiful quilt collection.

Avoncliff: Cross Guns Inn, spectacular setting on the south side of the aqueduct.

Bath: a long list of sights includes the Roman Baths and Pump Room, No 1 Royal Crescent (built by John Wood the Elder in 1768 and furnished in period), the Museum of Costume in the famous 18th-century Assembly Rooms, and buns in Sally Lunn's Refreshment House.

Bradford on Avon: Church of St Laurence, dated to 900 but hidden in amongst later buildings until 1856, is an almost complete Saxon church, its tall interior movingly plain.

Tithe Barn, one of the country's best medieval stone-built barns, originally belonging to

Shaftesbury Abbey (English Heritage).

The Courts, Holt, 2½ miles E of Bradford on Avon: a 7-acre 'garden of mystery' in the care of the National Trust.

Bristol: highlights include Brunel's SS Great Britain, the first iron-hulled ocean-going vessel and now the centrepiece of the revitalised docks area, the Exploratory Hands-On Science Centre (in Brunel's old Engine Shed at Temple Meads Station) for enquiring minds of all ages, and the City Museum and Art Gallery with displays of dinosaurs, ceramics, silver, natural history, etc.

Crofton Beam Engines, 7 miles E of Pewsey: the oldest working beam engine in the world, an 1812 Boulton and Watt, and an 1845 Harvey's of Hayle pump water into the Kennet & Avon with a 40ft lift; towpath walks.

Great Bedwyn: Stone Museum, a small but revealing insight into the ancient art of the stonemason.

Great Chalfield Manor, 3 miles E of Bradford on Avon: a mellow, late 15th-century moated house with a small 13th-century church (National Trust).

Kintbury: Dundas Arms, on a little island between the canal and the river overlooking Kintbury lock.

Reading: Blake's Lock Museum, in a Victorian pumping station, tells the part played by the waterways in Reading's industrial and commercial development.

Sandham Memorial Chapel, Burghclere, 4 miles S of Newbury: a First World War memorial chapel whose interior walls are covered with murals by Stanley Spencer depicting everyday wartime scenes (National Trust).

Westwood Manor, 1½ miles SW of Bradford on Avon: a 15th-century stone manor house, with original Jacobean plasterwork; modern topiary garden (National Trust).

The Grand Union Canal

and the Birmingham Canal Navigations

*L*IKE SO many others, I cut my canal teeth on the Grand Union. It was on this canal that I negotiated my first lock, drove a boat through my first tunnel and came to terms with the thousands of other activities and experiences that are intimately associated with inland waterways. It was this canal that taught me all about boats and their habits, and instilled in me, in common with everyone who enjoys canals, the desire to design the perfect boat. I started with a series of short outings on other people's boats, graduated to one-week holidays on hire craft exploring bits of the Grand Union and its connections, and finally did the whole London to Birmingham journey, an essential voyage through the heart of England and along the backbone of the inland waterway network. I remember how important it seemed to reach Birmingham and to get to grips with that city's vast and complex canal system. It was a kind of mecca, a barrier whose crossing represented a coming of age. It was familiarity with Gas Street Basin, the Engine Arm, Smethwick locks, the Rushall Canal, Dudley Port Junction, the Oozells Street loop and other such mysterious corners of the BCN, or the Birmingham Canal Navigations, to give this network its official title, that sorted the men from the boys.

My first visit to these infernal regions was at the end of a gloomy winter's afternoon when, after what seemed an eternity of travelling along a cutting whose wooded banks hid the world from

Two narrow boats leave Stoke Bruerne lock, travelling south, with the girls doing the work, as usual.

63

The Grand Union Canal

From the Thames at Brentford to Salford Junction in Birmingham
137 miles long, with 166 locks, all but 12 of which are broad
The Grand Union was the main line of a 300-mile network that linked London to Birmingham, Leicester and Nottingham, and included branches to many other towns *en route*.
Notable features Stoke Bruerne canal village, museum and locks, Blisworth tunnel, Braunston tunnel, locks and traditional narrow boats, Avon aqueduct in Leamington, Hatton flight of locks, Lapworth Junction and Stratford-on-Avon Canal, Knowle locks, Camp Hill locks.
History The Grand Union's origins lie in the late 18th-century Grand Junction Canal, a broad gauge waterway built to form a direct route from London to Birmingham, bypassing the old Oxford Canal and the Thames. The rapid success of the Grand Junction encouraged the opening of many branches along its Brentford to Braunston route, and other companies soon linked to it. A new canal was built from Braunston to Birmingham via Warwick and, at the London end, the Regent's Canal was opened from the Grand Junction's Paddington arm to Limehouse basin in the London docks, with a connection to the River Lee via the Hertford Union Canal. Other developments included the building of a canal from the Grand Junction to Leicester, Market Harborough, the River Soar and thus to the Trent, a route built in part, unfortunately, with conventional narrow locks, thus destroying the Grand Junction's hopes for a national broad gauge network. Profitable throughout the 19th century and into the 20th century, the Grand Junction was seen as one of the four British canals that could offer inland waterways a viable commercial future. As a result, the Grand Junction was the most important of a group of eight independent waterways merged in 1929 to form the Grand Union Canal Company. This new enterprise, whose network totalled over 300 miles and linked together London and the industrial centres of the Midlands, embarked immediately on a massive modernisation programme, backed by government finance. The 52 locks between Braunston and Birmingham were rebuilt to the broad gauge standard, bridges were enlarged and the canal itself was dredged and its banks

stabilised with concrete piles. Over £1 million was spent, but the scheme was never completed, and a new fleet of 66-ton capacity motor barges never went further than the experimental stage. Nevertheless, commercial transport survived on the Grand Union Canal until the 1970s, and nowadays it is one of the most popular cruising waterways in Britain.

The Birmingham Canal Navigations

The Black Country, the high plateau of the West Midlands that spreads from Birmingham and Stourbridge in the south to Wolverhampton and Cannock in the north, was at the very heart of the Industrial Revolution in Britain. From the early 18th century coal mining and metal industries dominated the landscape and gave the region its

Above: *The Delph flight of locks in the Dudley canal, a link between the Staffs & Worcs and the BCN.*

name. With no rivers of any significance, and the appalling roads over the hilly terrain, the region's economic life became dependent upon a remarkable network of canals. Then first, from Birmingham to Wednesbury, was opened in 1769, and from this there developed rapidly a compact and self-contained system which, at its peak in the mid-19th century, totalled over 160 miles. Within the system were over 500 narrow locks, three major tunnels, and innumerable bridges, aqueducts, basins and other structures built to serve the mines and factories of the Black Country. The system's extraordinary density, and its practicality as a short haul network, enabled it to continue in commercial operation well into the 1960s. Today, about 100 miles of the BCN still

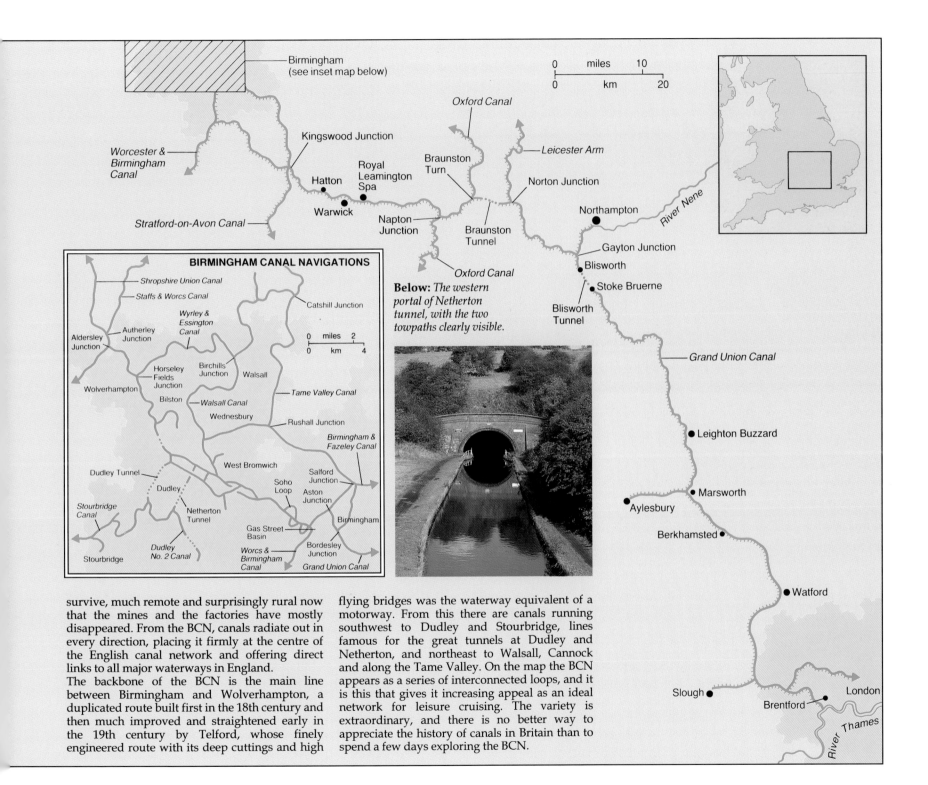

Birmingham
(see inset map below)

Oxford Canal

Worcester &
Birmingham
Canal

Kingswood Junction

Leicester Arm

Braunston
Turn

Royal
Leamington
Spa

Norton Junction

Hatton

Warwick

Napton
Junction

Braunston
Tunnel

Northampton

River Nene

Gayton Junction

Blisworth

Stratford-on-Avon Canal

Oxford Canal

Stoke Bruerne

Blisworth
Tunnel

Below: *The western portal of Netherton tunnel, with the two towpaths clearly visible.*

BIRMINGHAM CANAL NAVIGATIONS

Shropshire Union Canal

Staffs & Worcs Canal

Catshill Junction

Wyrley &
Essington
Canal

Aldersley
Junction

Autherley
Junction

Horseley
Fields
Junction

Birchills
Junction

Walsall

Wolverhampton

Bilston

Walsall Canal

Tame Valley Canal

Wednesbury

Rushall Junction

Birmingham &
Fazeley Canal

Dudley Tunnel

West Bromwich

Salford
Junction

Dudley

Soho
Loop

Aston
Junction

Stourbridge
Canal

Netherton
Tunnel

Birmingham

Gas Street
Basin

Stourbridge

Dudley
No. 2 Canal

Worcs &
Birmingham
Canal

Bordesley
Junction

Grand Union Canal

Grand Union Canal

Leighton Buzzard

Marsworth

Aylesbury

Berkhamsted

Watford

Slough

Brentford

London

River Thames

survive, much remote and surprisingly rural now that the mines and the factories have mostly disappeared. From the BCN, canals radiate out in every direction, placing it firmly at the centre of the English canal network and offering direct links to all major waterways in England.

The backbone of the BCN is the main line between Birmingham and Wolverhampton, a duplicated route built first in the 18th century and then much improved and straightened early in the 19th century by Telford, whose finely engineered route with its deep cuttings and high flying bridges was the waterway equivalent of a motorway. From this there are canals running southwest to Dudley and Stourbridge, lines famous for the great tunnels at Dudley and Netherton, and northeast to Walsall, Cannock and along the Tame Valley. On the map the BCN appears as a series of interconnected loops, and it is this that gives it increasing appeal as an ideal network for leisure cruising. The variety is extraordinary, and there is no better way to appreciate the history of canals in Britain than to spend a few days exploring the BCN.

Above: *The heart of the BCN
is the canal from Birmingham
north to Wolverhampton. On
the left is Telford's new main
line, while the original main
line is on the right, at a higher
level. In the centre is the
restored Smethwick pumping
station.*

Opposite: *Gas Street Basin
at the centre of Birmingham.*

view, we finally reached an open landscape of
industrial dereliction and old warehouses. A long,
empty straight took us to the top of the Camp Hill
flight of locks. Dark, oily and generally
insalubrious, these locks dropped the canal down
under a confusion of old railway bridges to
Bordesley Junction, the official end of the Grand
Union. From here onwards it was the secret and
arcane world of the BCN. We plunged on into the
gathering darkness, our boundaries defined by the
black encompassing walls that seemed to isolate the
canal from reality. Increasingly in a dream world,
we climbed up lock flights, carved our way through
dark and sinister bridges, and passed by branch
canals that ran off to inconceivable destinations.
The only boats we saw were the distant shapes of
old iron barges, half hidden in forgotten corners.
Occasionally figures on the towpath would loom
out of the darkness, quickly to be swallowed up
again. For all we knew, they might have been
ghosts, dimly populating some 19th-century world

into which we had been plunged. At some point we
stopped, and sat for a while in a pub filled, it
seemed to us, with old boatmen speaking in
impenetrable Black Country voices. It all became
rather hazy after that, but we must have travelled
on, as the night was spent moored beneath Snow
Hill railway station.

After that first visit, the BCN had a hold, and I
revisited it many times, on a number of occasions
reducing friends to silence by telling them that I
was spending my holidays touring Birmingham by
boat. Bit by bit every corner was explored, every
junction, every lock, every bridge, mostly by boat,
but sometimes on foot. The most obscure parts I
visited by motorcycle (normally forbidden, but I
had been been given a special permit by British
Waterways in order to do the research needed for a
waterway guide). Although it was not strictly
necessary, I could not resist the challenge of driving
my bike through the darkness of the Great
Netherton tunnel, one of the few with the luxury of
a towpath, and I lived to tell the tale. In those days
the BCN was a secret world indeed, the whole
network largely cut off from the normality of
Birmingham up above, and accessible from the
streets in only a few places, where a door in a wall,
or a dark alleyway could suddenly take you on to
the towpath. One doorway led us, via an old set of
steps in patterned blue brick, to the famous Gas
Street Basin. Now a busy marina overlooked by
flashy modern buildings and smart restaurants, and
much photographed by visiting trippers, in those
days Gas Street was a very private world, a step
back into the shadows of a dimly remembered past.
Completely surrounded by the dark towering walls
of old warehouses, the basin, filled with traditional
narrow boats, was a sight never to be forgotten. The
drifting smoke from the boat chimneys and the
gloomy half light softened the patterned colours
and the edges of the cabins into a ghostly
insubstantiality. There was the smell of the coke
fires, and in the distance a radio was quietly
playing some ill-defined dance band tune.

Time-travellers, we lurked in the grey shadows, watching the magic, but not wanting to break the spell and, after a while, we climbed back to the normality of the city street at night.

The inhabitants of this underworld, the last survivors of the once great tribe of commercial boatmen, were then still at work and on the BCN a pleasure cruiser was a rarer sight than a traditional narrow boat or an elderly tug towing a pair of iron barges filled with the most basic and dirty cargoes. Today all this has largely gone, and the BCN has found its place in the changing world of leisure. Boatyards and marinas have appeared, and the towpaths have become urban walkways, with access not only easy but encouraged by official signs in the streets. The BCN now plays its part in bringing tourism to Birmingham and the Black Country, but the magic does live on. There is still nothing like it to excite the imagination, and no better way of coming to terms with the vitality of the canals in their heyday. It remains a huge network, despite the miles of branches, basins and alternative routes that have been obliterated in this century, and, as every guide book writer knows, there are still more canals in Birmingham than there are in Venice.

Above: *The boater's view of the M5 motorway.*
Left: *Climbing up the Farmer's Bridge flight.*

Opposite: *Dudley Port Junction, where the Netherton tunnel branch leaves the main line.*

My own boat, when I came to buy one, came naturally from a Black Country boatyard, a tough, sturdy vessel, hardly elegant but carrying in its chunky lines centuries of practical canal experience. And I have never regretted that decision.

The canal boat is a distinct species of craft, quite apart from the normal conventions of the maritime world. Its design evolved out of practical necessity, determined as much as anything by the size and shape of the locks through which it had to pass. By the early 19th century a standard type of vessel had emerged, about 70ft long and 7ft wide, with much

Above: *A traditional narrow boat from the Fellows, Morton and Clayton fleet of canal carriers, converted for domestic use. It is painted in the FMC colours and has characteristic brass fittings. The smaller, brass bound chimney takes the exhaust from the diesel engine, which would originally have been a massive Bolinder single-cylinder motor.*

of its length an open box into which all kinds of cargo could be loaded. Empty, it rode slab-sided, high out of the water; loaded, it sailed with only a few inches of freeboard, for waves on canals are few and far between. 'Sailed' is hardly a suitable word, for the boat was dragged through the water by a horse or horses, donkeys, occasionally an unlikely pairing of horse and donkey, or by teams of men. It had a steerer, placed at the stern, behind the most rudimentary of shelters. Construction was generally of wood, but iron and steel gradually took over as those materials developed. It had to be strongly built to survive innumerable, and inevitable, collisions with lock gates and walls, the sides of bridges and tunnels, and with other craft. Wider versions were made for wider canals and river navigations, and those designed for coastal and estuary work, as well as inland navigation, were built to be more seaworthy.

In the 19th century the cabins became larger and better equipped as the crew, and then whole families, began to live on board. With the arrival of self-propulsion, the narrow boats were grouped into pairs, one of which was fitted with an engine. This towed the other, the butty, and together they could carry about 50 tons, crewed by two or three people, or one family. Until the Second World War, this was a cheap, reliable and practical form of inland transport, particularly over short distances and, although canals did suffer from railway competition, it was really the rapid development of motor transport from the 1930s onwards that killed them.

The tradition of family-based boating evolved a whole culture of its own, affecting social habits, language, dress and food, along with a wealth of decoration. The habit of living on a narrow boat for a lifetime produced characteristic ways of improving, and making more domestic, the basic environment of the boat and its cabin. These included particular ways with rope, and a range of cabin fittings whose intricacy matched those of a gypsy caravan. Best known, however, are the styles of painting, both in the treatment of wooden surfaces with graining and in the multi-coloured decorations that used typical peasant-like images of flowers, landscapes and castles, balanced by beautifully inventive sign writing. Also typical is the extensive use of highly polished brass.

When the world of canals began, from the 1930s, to attract the attention of outsiders, it was these decorative features that were seized upon. The first generation of canal enthusiasts bought and operated traditional narrow boats, enjoying greatly their colourful decoration and their range of painted metal fittings, such as the water container and its matching dipper. The next generation began to move away from the narrow boats, finding them expensive to maintain and complicated to operate on a network where standards of maintenance were slipping. Driving a 70ft boat does require a certain kind of expertise, particularly on a narrow and

first-ever canal trip, along the Oxford Canal, was in a plastic boat. We were certainly not careless, but it was windy, and the boat gradually fell to pieces around us, unable to cope with the normal buffeting that any canal boat has to endure. Panels and screens fell off, and every time we had to give a firm pull on a rope, the cleat holding it flew off the plastic hull. The outboard motor was constantly choked by weeds and debris, and consumed a staggering amount of petrol to achieve a very limited progress through the water. The material is totally unsuitable, and yet the canals are still full of plastic boats, driven along by cocky chaps with blondes and yachting caps whose cheery grins give way to blind panic every time they have to negotiate a lock. Hundreds of fenders, miles of ropes, and plenty of shouting are the natural accompaniments to this event, with the whole process carried out at a snail's pace.

The only practical modern canal boat is the custom-built steel cruiser, and these are made in every length from 15ft to 70ft, and to all standards of finish by boatyards all over Britain. Tough, and with reliable diesel engines, these can survive the most appalling abuse at the hands of first-time

twisting canal with very restricted bridges and locks, and anyone who has stood on the stern of such a vessel, holding the tiller, will know how far away the bow seems to be. More importantly, the major part of any traditional narrow boat is, of course, the empty hold, and so for social or pleasure use the cabin is ridiculously small. At first, the hold was converted into extra accommodation, but this was never a perfect solution to the problem.

Another solution was to adapt pleasure cruisers that had been built for river use, but this was also generally unsatisfactory as they were usually too wide and too deep draughted. None the less, some quite extraordinary looking and remarkably unseaworthy vessels were to be seen happily cruising Britain's canals during the 1950s and early 1960s. The ex-army wooden bridge pontoon was the basis for many such craft, propelled along by an ancient and smoky outboard motor. Next came the first batch of custom-built boats, designed with canals in mind. Initially wooden, but increasingly made from plastics, these proliferated during the 1960s, but were usually woefully inadequate. My

Above: *A traditional narrow boat cabin in Stoke Bruerne Canal Museum.*

Below: *Boat building at Braunston.*

hirers, and still give plenty of pleasure. The fittings can range from basic to super luxurious. I remember an extreme example of the latter category, modelled by its architect owner on Hugh Heffner's private jet. Shown round by the paid hand, we examined the grand bath, the central heating, the deep sofas, the fully equipped kitchen, the sun terrace and the water bed. With every refinement to self-indulgence, this boat could still fit through an ordinary narrow lock.

The real problem with modern boats is that their owners like to pretend that they have a traditional narrow boat, and so perfectly pleasant and attractive craft are often defaced by 'traditional style' paintwork, complete with stick-on transfers of roses and castles, curiously out of step with the televisions, chintzy cushions and shag-pile carpets that lurk within.

There are, of course, centres of traditional canal life, sometimes in the fantasy world of museums and theme parks, but more often in the more obscure parts of the canal network, where that dwindling number of die-hard enthusiasts who continue to maintain and operate traditional narrow boats come together. One such place is Braunston, a village famous in the story of the Grand Union. Historically complicated, the Grand Union is well named, for it was formed in the 1920s to link together a series of independent canals whose routes connected London with Birmingham, Nottingham and Leicester. The first, and most important, of these was the Grand Junction, a late 18th-century scheme to construct a canal to London from Braunston that would offer a route from the Midlands that bypassed the meandering Oxford Canal and the River Thames. Built with broad 14ft locks, it reduced the distance by some 60 miles and was immediately successful, prompting the construction of a series of arms and branches to link towns such as Aylesbury and Buckingham to the network. The promoters of this canal hoped that other companies would be encouraged to rebuild their waterways to the 14ft standard. Had this

happened, the story of British canals could well have been very different, but in the event shortage of money and a lack of imagination meant that James Brindley's 7ft narrow locks remained the standard. Other canals inspired by the success of the Grand Junction included one to connect it to Birmingham via Warwick, a route to Market Harborough and Leicester to join the River Soar Navigation and thus the Trent and, at the London end, links to the Thames and the River Lee. This huge network, the backbone of the English canal system, was merged into the Grand Union Canal Company, and a massive, but somewhat belated, modernisation programme was launched, helped by government money. The route from London was improved, and the locks between Braunston and Birmingham were widened to the 14ft standard.

With its wide locks, generous bridges and tall embankments, the Grand Union is a magnificently engineered waterway. Like Brunel's Great Western

Above: *Traditional narrow boats at Stoke Bruerne. The* Brighton *and the* Fazeley, *with their characteristic upswept tillers, are butties, and in the centre is a motor boat. Originally they would have operated as pairs, each motor towing a butty.*

Opposite: *A colourful display of modern and traditional narrow boats at Braunston marina.*

Above: *Stoke Bruerne top lock, with the village and the Canal Museum in the background.*

Opposite: *A narrow boat emerging into the daylight from the southern end of Blisworth tunnel.*

Railway, it has a generosity of scale that hints at how things might have been if those who planned it had had their way throughout the English network. Anyone travelling the canal for the first time cannot fail to be aware of this, continually underlined as it is by the engineering. Particularly exciting and impressive are the tunnels, the greatest of which is at Blisworth, a good place to start an exploration of the Grand Union. At the tunnel's southern end is Stoke Bruerne, an ideal canal village, at the head of a flight of locks, with traditional stone cottages, an old church, a suitably rural pub, and a waterways museum. The only thing that spoils it is its obvious popularity, and anyone working their boat up the locks had better be on their metal, for the top lock is always ringed by spectators keen to observe bungles and failures of technique, and to pass remarks of a generally unhelpful nature.

The tunnel entrance is half a mile away, a great hole in the hill wide enough for two narrow boats to pass. Over 3,000yds in length, it is the longest navigable canal tunnel in Britain. There is nothing to match the excitement of one's first tunnel, and to disappear for half an hour or more into the dark is always memorable. The only light comes from the boat's headlamp, a yellow beam made circular by the reflection from the water. Even the brightest light seems to show only a short section of the irregular rocky or brick-lined walls, and behind there is nothing but impenetrable blackness, with the grey shadow of the mouth steadily diminishing. Ahead there will eventually be the pinhole of light that is the other mouth, but for a very long while it never seems to get any bigger. Steering is deceptively difficult, the tricks of the light making the walls appear to come in and out, and echoing bumps are not uncommon. The engine thumps, filling the space, and if you meet another boat, the noise is deafening. First you see the round disc of yellow light, then you come together and pass, with a few shouted remarks between boats, and then it is swallowed again by the blackness. The roof drips continuously, and sometimes streams with water, and the steerer soon discovers another basic and inflexible rule of canal life, namely that regardless of skill or steered course, the water will always fall down the neck. A broad-brimmed hat is the only answer. Long tunnels have air vents, shafts cut vertically up to the top of the hill far above, and you pass quickly through the circles of grey light that they project on to the water. A friend, who shall be nameless, celebrated a Guy Fawkes Night afloat by firing rockets up the air shafts of a certain tunnel, and by letting off bangers which caused spectacular reverberations through the tunnel. It was highly entertaining down below, but the effects on the surface above are not recorded.

North of Blisworth is Gayton Junction, where the branch to Northampton and the River Nene drops away down a long flight of locks. This is followed by another junction where the canal to Leicester swings away to the northeast, a heavily locked route whose start can be examined at leisure from

the Watford Gap service area on the M1 motorway. Then comes another great tunnel. This is Braunston, a mere 2,042yds long, but made exciting by the famous kink in the middle which makes it impossible to see right through and therefore deceptively long and dark. At the tunnel's north end is the flight of locks that takes the canal down to Braunston, always a canal village and now a mecca for traditional narrow boat owners and builders. From here to Napton, about 5 miles away, the Grand Union shares its route with the Oxford Canal, this older and much slower waterway soon leaving to start its steep climb up Napton Hill.

The big locks of the Grand Union now come thick and fast, dropping the canal down into the Avon Valley, through Leamington Spa, and round to the east of Warwick. An aqueduct carries it over the Avon, and then it starts the big climb up to Birmingham. In the way are the 21 Hatton locks, the most impressive and certainly the most daunting flight in England. Hatton is a challenge that every boater has to face sooner or later, and the sight of these great locks, rising one after another, and apparently without end, is something to make the toughest among us turn pale. Others may consider giving up canals for good. A personal vision of hell would be climbing Hatton in wind and rain for ever. The locks seem huge, high-walled and unforgiving, the gates are heavy and have a life of their own, and the distinctive paddle gear, a patent type introduced during the 1930s modernisation programme, require an incalculable amount of winding to operate. I have done Hatton many times, up and down, and, like everyone in this position, I have my personal best time for the flights, which I always hope to beat but never do. Once, nearly 20 years ago, on a good day, and with locks in our favour, we did it in about 2 ½ hours. The secret is in the teamwork. The boat steerer, preferably a woman, for women are good at this

The Hatton flight of locks is exhausting. Particularly tiring is the distinctive winding gear of its paddles.

particular and demandingly precise skill, has to have a perfect sense of timing and control. The two on the land have also to be well co-ordinated, one always up ahead getting the next lock ready, the other staying with the boat to get it quickly through the lock. The one who goes ahead is called the lock wheeler, because this activity is achieved most successfully with a bicycle, an essential piece of boat equipment. In the course of the Hatton flight, this shore party will walk and run miles, and at the end even the fittest will be on their knees. My many Hatton experiences have included a long delay caused by a fallen tree, being continually driven aground between locks by high winds, having to return for a stranded dog and, one sunny autumn morning, being threatened with a terrible fate by my shore party who had been compelled to complete the flight before I served breakfast. I drove them onwards relentlessly, my best time in my mind. The only reason I escaped with my life, or at least without a ducking, was that they were too exhausted. And we failed to beat the time. On another occasion, teamwork went too far. There were four adults in the party and two four-year-old children. Leaving a lock, the steerer, believing another adult to be below, put the boat into gear and got off to close the top gate. The boat sailed slowly on into the next pound, and at that point four adults found themselves on the lockside, watching its departing stern. It was a serious case of 'don't panic'. Shouting raised the children on to the deck from their activities below and one of them grasped the tiller and steered successfully to the next lock upon shouted instructions of the 'this way a bit' and 'that way a bit' variety from his father, despite being far too small to see where he was going. The other child, his twin sister, also took it in good part, as a harmless piece of adult eccentricity, letting them have a go at steering on their own.

Left: *Camp Hill locks drop the Grand Union Canal into the heart of Birmingham.*

From Hatton it is all plain sailing, relatively speaking. At Lapworth a short arm links the Grand Union to the Stratford-on-Avon Canal, whose wandering route provides a more salubrious way into Birmingham, plus the added delights of the long King's Norton tunnel. There are more broad Grand Union locks at Knowle, but hardened veterans of Hatton will do these in their sleep, and then it is straight on to Birmingham, through that city's suburbs, initially desirable, but increasingly less so as the journey progresses. Luckily much of the route is in a cutting, and so only the rubbish thrown down into the canal by the locals gives clues to the changing nature of the surroundings. By the end of the cutting, the setting is definitely industrial, and then the narrow Camp Hill locks announce the start of Birmingham proper. And that is where we came in . . .

Right: *A traditional cast iron towpath bridge near Farmer's Bridge, Birmingham, overshadowed by the National Indoor Sports Arena.*

PLACES TO VISIT
Baddesley Clinton, Knowle, 1½ miles NE of Kingswood: a romantic medieval moated house, little changed since 1634; family portraits, priest holes, ponds and lake walk (National Trust).
Birmingham: an extensive list of sights includes Aston Hall, a Jacobean mansion with a splendid Long Gallery, the Barber Institute of Fine Arts, the Birmingham Nature Centre for beavers, deer and much else, Blakesley Hall, an Elizabethan farmhouse furnished in period, the Botanical Gardens and Glasshouses, Cadbury World at Bournville for a chocolate experience, the City Museum & Art Gallery for its pre-Raphaelite collection, Perrott's Folly for the view, Selly Manor Museum in Bournville, two reconstructed manor houses with herb gardens, the Railway Museum, Sarehole Mill, a working 18th-century water mill that was inspiration for J R R Tolkien's *The Hobbit*, and the ruins of 13th-century Weoley Castle.
Dudley: Black Country Museum, a Victorian Black Country village re-created on the canal bank, with costumed guides, tramway rides, canal trips into the Dudley tunnel.
Zoo and Castle, a traditional zoo in wooded castle grounds.
Kingswood: The Navigation, classic pub in a tranquil setting with popular canalside garden.
Northampton: Abington Park Museum, reconstructed period street, toys.
Central Museum & Art Gallery, focuses on the shoe making industry with a varied collection of shoes and boots.
Museum of Leathercraft tells the story from Egyptian times to today.
Old Dairy Farm Centre, Weedon Bec, near Upper Stowe: rare breeds, craft workshops and outlets, housed in converted farm buildings around a working arable and sheep farm.
Packwood House, Lapworth, 2 miles NW of Kingswood: Tudor house with fine tapestries, needlework, furniture and Jacobean panelling; 17th-century yew garden clipped to depict Christ's Sermon on the Mount (National Trust).
Royal Leamington Spa: Royal Pump Rooms and Regency terraces, overlooking Jephson Gardens' bordered walks, lakes and aviary.
Art Gallery & Museum, displaying paintings, porcelain and glass.
Solihull: the National Motorcycle Museum displays British motorcycles from the Golden Age of motorcycling.
Stoke Bruerne: Canal Museum has three floors of bygones from two centuries of canals, including the reconstructed interior of a traditional narrow boat; boat trips through Blisworth tunnel.
Boat Inn, thatched pub that plays its part in this picturesque canal village.
Warwick: places of interest include the massive 14th-century castle with Old Masters in the magnificent state rooms and grisly tortures in the dungeons; the Church of St Mary's, of Norman origin; the County Museum housing the Sheldon 1588 tapestry map of Warwickshire; the Doll Museum in 16th-century Oken's House; Lord Leycester Hospital, a 14th-century half-timbered building housing almshouses and the Regimental Museum of the Queen's Own Hussars.

The Staffordshire and Worcestershire Canal

CRUISING a popular waterway like the Staffs & Worcs during the summer gives ample opportunity to observe the habits of people on other boats. Notable above all else is the frenetic pace at which so many, particularly those on hired boats, seem to need to lead their lives. Their boats pass at full speed, leaving a wash that visibly eats away the banks of the canal. The males of the party are invariably at the controls, relaxing, eating and drinking, and chatting amongst themselves while the women get on with exactly the same chores that they do at home, washing, tidying, cooking, shopping and looking after the children. The holiday for them is presumably the extra duties, the walking a long way to unfamiliar shops, the worrying about water supplies and the lavatories, and the tasks imposed by the canal itself. It is a familiar scene, the large steel boat racing towards a lock whose wooden gates are firmly closed. At the last moment the shell-suited slouch at the tiller slings the boat into reverse and amid noise and smoke and thrashing water it shudders to a halt. In the meantime his devoted family slaves have flung themselves towards the land, bravely, and quite unnecessarily, risking all as they leap across huge distances clutching tangled ropes. They wind up the paddles and open and close the gates, tiring exercises at the best of times and sometimes ones that demand a great deal of physical strength, while their man rests on the tiller and has another beer. The boat rises or falls, gates open, the women leap

Early 19th-century canalside buildings at Stourport, in the typical soft red Worcestershire brick.

The Staffordshire and Worcestershire Canal

From Stourport on the River Severn to Great Haywood on the Trent and Mersey Canal
46 miles long, with 31 locks spread throughout the route

Notable features Stourport locks, basins and canal architecture, Kidderminster for Severn Valley Railway, Cookley locks and tunnel, sandstone cliffs and rocks around Cookley and Kinver, Bratch locks, Great Haywood bridge and junction.

History Planned as part of the engineer James Brindley's network of trunk canals to link the main rivers of Britain, the Staffordshire and Worcestershire was completed in 1772. The construction costs were in excess of £100,000, yet there was no shortage of investors who could see the potential the canal offered for improving the transport links between the new areas of industry and the ports. They were not disappointed, and the canal was quickly busy and profitable. Rival routes were opened, notably the more direct Worcester and Birmingham Canal in 1815, and later the Birmingham and Liverpool Junction Company also joined the fray. Despite these, and the ever-increasing railway network, the Staffs and Worcs continued to operate profitably and paid dividends to its shareholders throughout the 19th century. Unlike most of its rivals and neighbours, it never sold out to the railway companies, and retained its independence right up until the whole canal network was nationalised by the government in 1947. By that time it was an obscure and little-used waterway, devoid of commercial traffic, and yet retaining its particular atmosphere and quality. Never modernised or enlarged, the Staffs and Worcs today offers the chance to see an 18th-century canal which is in a relatively original condition and whose contribution to its fine landscape surroundings has always been positive.

Above: *A quiet mooring for a modern narrow boat below Wolverley lock.*

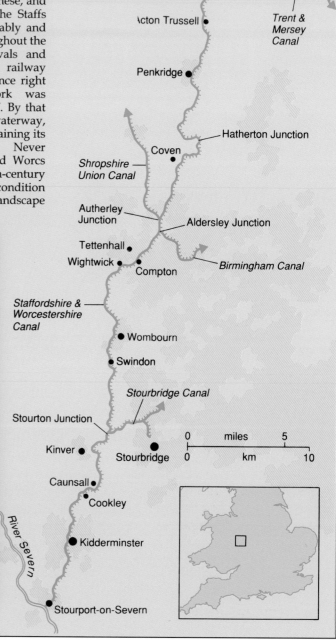

back on and return to their domestic duties, and the engine bellows again at full throttle as the boat races off.

Despite all this turmoil and activity, the actual speed of such a boat along its route is still little more than a walking pace even when there are no locks. The passage through a lock can take anything between five and 15 minutes and so over a long journey on a typical British canal it is reasonable to expect an average speed of 1½ miles per hour. This is a speed determined by such elements as the depth of water, the number of curves and the amount of traffic as well as locks, bridges and tunnels. Driving at full throttle actually has little effect upon the equation, merely creating noise and aggravation. A canal imposes its own pace and its own way of life, and this is why a journey should be such a relaxing change from normal daily pressures. Anyone bringing these pressures with them and imposing them on the environment of the canal should have stayed at home.

The temptation to get as far as possible, as quickly as possible, in a given period of time, whether it be a weekend, a week or a fortnight, is hard to resist, and I have fallen prey to it on a number of occasions. It is the inevitability of such desires that has brought into being a series of circular routes within the network that can be completed, without undue stress, within these time limits. Such routes were always there, but were irrelevant to boaters whose sole aim was to carry cargo from one point to another by the best means. Certain routes, understandably popular, are over-used, while others, for various reasons, are under-used. It is also inevitable that some of the most popular are also the most delicate and delightful canals, canals which are being ground down by constant use and abuse, mindless or otherwise.

The Staffordshire & Worcestershire Canal is one of these. For anyone seeking out the typical British canal, this would be an excellent candidate. It is old, having been opened as early as 1772, it has all the

features that make the canals of this period so appealing, a wandering route through an attractive landscape in which the canal itself is an important element, plenty of examples of exciting 18th-century engineering including lock flights, tunnels, cuttings and other impressive works, fine architecture built with that instinctive eye for quality that characterised the engineers of both the canal and the railway networks, interesting things to see along the route and an intimate view of a part of England whose traditional virtues survive despite the proximity of so much industrial development. It is a slow canal, built at a time when

Above: *At Stourton Junction a lock connects the Staffs & Worcs and the Stourbridge canals, a peaceful scene despite the proximity of Birmingham.*

Above: *Gailey lock with the unusual circular lock-keeper's house.*

Opposite: *Leaving Filance lock on the way to Penkridge.*

even the slowest passage of a boat along a waterway was still an incredible improvement over all other transport systems, and today speed is entirely limited by its sinuous path through the landscape, its narrow cuttings and above all else by its aged locks. It is a pleasure that has to be taken slowly, a gentle seduction rather than violent rape.

Engineered by James Brindley, and planned as part of that first group of 18th-century artery canals that were to connect the four great commercial rivers of England, the Severn, the Thames, the Trent and the Mersey, the Staffs & Worcs represented the link between the Severn and the Mersey, via Brindley's major enterprise, the recently completed Trent & Mersey Canal. From Stourport on the Severn to Great Haywood on the Trent & Mersey, it was the nearest to a straight line that 18th-century engineering could achieve. Hard to appreciate today for those looking at the Severn's wide emptiness and massive but little-used locks is the vital role played by that river in the economy of 18th-century Britain. At that time it was fully navigable to Ironbridge and beyond, and the characteristic craft, the Severn trows, plied their way up and down the river, carrying the raw materials and products of industry between centres such as Ironbridge and the ports of Bristol and South Wales. Such was the scale of both local and international trade that the Severn was simply not enough, and so by the 1760s the need for cross-country links between the river and the manufacturing centres of the Midlands and north was widely appreciated. The great canal trunk routes were seen as the answer to this need, and the last decades of the 18th century witnessed the planning and construction of canals that made possible through navigation between London, Bristol and South Wales, the Midlands, Liverpool and the Northeast. Brindley was a key figure, being responsible for the planning of much of the network, and for launching the transport revolution that made possible the dynamic industrial and economic expansion of late 18th-century Britain.

The scale of the enterprise and the imagination that inspired it is hard to grasp today but, by comparison, the Channel Tunnel is a rabbit burrow. It is curious that it was the same James Brindley who, by one vital error, also doomed the waterway network to a much shorter commercial life than its European equivalents. It was he who determined that the standard lock size for the canals of Britain should be 72ft by 7ft, despite the fact that much larger locks already existed in river navigations in many parts of the country. He was influenced by cost and, more importantly, by the problems of water supply. He knew that Britain lacked the great rivers of Europe that kept canals full of water even during the driest conditions, and so the only way to ensure sufficient supplies of water to keep traffic moving was to build small locks, and as few as possible, fed by a combination of existing water sources and reservoirs. At the time, the dimension he chose must have seemed generous enough, allowing as it did the passage of boats carrying between 20 and 30 tons. Now, we can see that right from the start the new canals of Britain were too small. It was as though Robert Stephenson, instead of selecting the railway gauge of 4ft 8½ ins that became standard throughout much of the world, had chosen instead something much narrower, and in the process doomed Britain to a network of miniature railways. The Staffs & Worcs is just such a narrow canal, and it is its small scale, a factor which ultimately destroyed its commercial life, that gives it so much appeal today.

In general terms, the canal network survived until the Second World War as a national transport enterprise, and then the decline, whose roots were in the late Victorian period, was unexpectedly rapid. Commercial life staggered on through the 1950s, dwindling rapidly and then was dead in practical terms by the early 1960s. It is said that the harsh winters of 1947 and 1963, when the whole system was frozen solid for weeks, were the deathblows, but they were really only the *coup de grâce* for a whole way of life that was no longer required.

The disappearance of commercial carrying brought the canal network to the brink of closure, and indeed in the early 1960s many canals were formally abandoned. The charging of tolls had always been the network's financial heart, and when these went there was no immediate way to generate the income required for maintenance and support. Pleasure boating was still in its infancy, and there was none of the current enthusiasm for leisure. The general view was that canals were, like steam trains, dinosaurs from another age, and that both should, accordingly, be allowed to die. The irony of course is that both have survived, kept alive by the unexpected infusion of a new kind of life blood. In the 1950s it was inconceivable to imagine either that leisure could become a major national enterprise, or that the whole British way of life would turn backwards, to wallow in some nostalgic and wholly fanciful re-creation of the past. Today, steam trains in rich profusion meander aimlessly along remote stretches of track all over Britain, from Cornwall to the north of Scotland, undertaking journeys whose only purpose is the entertainment of the passengers, a perfect example of virtual reality established long before that concept was actually born. By the same token, canals still spread their twisting routes through England, Wales and even parts of Scotland, and these routes are filled with boats making journeys that, by the traditional rules of canal life, are completely pointless. The pleasure is in the journey and the route, and removed completely is the necessity actually to get anywhere. Many canals are now busier in traffic terms than they were during the 19th century, but this traffic does not really pay its way. Maintenance and support has now to be centrally funded and, in this post-Thatcher era everyone knows what that means. Revenue is certainly generated by the licensing of pleasure craft, but this produces a small fraction of the total required. Far more significant are sales of water and land, property development and other activities only indirectly connected to the canals themselves.

The result, of course, is a heavily used system whose maintenance is under-funded, and whose age is apparent at every point. The appeal of the canals is exactly this, an old-fashioned, even archaic, and delightfully rural network that offers the perfect escape. However, like all old things, it has to be treated with great care. Abuse merely hastens its demise. In the days of regular commercial traffic there were schedules and timetables, and boat crews were compelled to work long hours in difficult conditions in order to maintain them. At the same time, there was an infrastructure of maintenance and support throughout the canal network that was designed to cope with the demands on the system imposed by this way of life. Modern boaters, travelling only for the sake of the journey itself, have other needs, and the use they impose on the network is very different, and ultimately more demanding and destructive. Thrashing a boat along mindlessly at

Below: *A busy scene at the Bratch staircase locks, a popular spot for boat watching.*

top speed is canal abuse of the worst kind, for it destroys not only the peace and quiet engendered by the canal but also the canal itself. Bridges, tunnels, the earthworks that support them, and locks are delicate and elderly things, easily damaged by those who treat them without care or respect.

Working a boat gently through narrow locks is always a pleasure, regardless of the setting and even the weather. The clanking iron of the old paddles, the wooden balance beams and the creaking gates all bring the canal age to life in a very direct way. It is hard not to think of the thousands of boats that have passed through, and the people they carried, many of whom have known no other home than the cramped cabin of a narrow boat. Imagine two adults and up to three children living all their lives in a space about 10ft by 7ft, and any romantic illusions about the realities of canal life will soon evaporate. The locks are the most tangible reminders of the canals in their heyday, for nothing has changed. The effort involved in winding up the paddles is exactly as it was two centuries ago, and so the realities of operating a traditional canal boat can be readily imagined, even if the life itself is beyond recall.

The dangers involved in operating locks have not changed either. Most accidents happen at locks, and there are plenty of ways of causing harm to yourself or the boat. You can start with falling in, easily done while crossing the gates to operate the lock, especially when it is wet, dark or icy. The experience is unpleasant, not necessarily lethal, but climbing out of the bottom of an empty lock, early on a cold morning, with heavy wet clothes, is not something easily forgotten. Falling in is probably an essential learning exercise, and it always happens at the most inconvenient time and at difficult places. Lock gates, gangplanks, the narrow walkways along the wides of boats, are all things that can, without warning, tip you into the water. The lock machinery is also hazardous if treated with insufficient respect. Fingers get crushed, clothing

caught or covered in grease, and there is always the possibility of causing a hernia while struggling with particularly heavy and unfriendly paddles. It is a common habit to leave the windlass on the crank and go off for a chat while the lock fills or empties. Such windlasses can, unexpectedly, cause the rachet to slip, at which point they rotate at ever increasing speed, breaking everything that comes in their way, or flying off completely along a huge and unpredictable parabola that seems always to send a piece of iron at your head, wherever you are standing. Things can go wrong in operating the lock itself. Gates and paddles have a life of their own and can jam for no apparent reason. Using the paddles in the wrong order can cause interesting floods and serious water wastage. The gates at the back of each lock sit on a sill that sticks forward into the water. It is therefore all too easy, in an emptying lock, to stick the stern of the boat on the sill. The first thing you will know of it will be your boat adopting a serious, and rapidly increasing, downhill slant. Frantic shouting may solve the crisis, but by one of those great universal laws your

Above: *Opening the paddles in the bottom gates of Kidderminster lock, to allow the water to fall.*

companion up on the lock side will have chosen this moment to go for a pee, or to talk to someone in a distant field. This is one of the many ways you can sink your boat, but only rarely does it come to so drastic a conclusion. Another way is to flood the boat from above, by the careless opening into an empty lock of the paddle sometimes found in the centre of the top gate. This releases a veritable Niagara, most of which is bound, by another universal law, to go straight into the boat. I remember one such occasion, when this tidal wave tore through the boat towards the stern, where I was innocently leaning on the tiller, contemplating the dripping brickwork. For some reason I decided to handle this crisis by leaping on to the roof and rushing towards the bow; irrational behaviour at the best of times, and in direct contravention of the first law of canal boat life Never run! When I came to the end of the roof I slipped, and fell into the well in the bow from which one watches the passing scenery. Various hard and sharp pieces of steel broke my fall, causing deep pain in many parts, a pain that was made much worse both by the accompanying rage and by the discovery that I was lying exactly where the Niagara was hitting the boat. In the event this, like most canal crises, was somehow brought to an end without any lasting damagebeing done. My scars eventually healed, and the carpets eventually dried.

The Staffs & Worcs starts at Stourport, an 18th-century town created entirely to serve the needs of the canal. Brindley originally planned to connect his canal to the Severn at Bewdley, an established river port, but that town did not want it, and so he made the junction instead at a remote spot where the little River Stour joined the Severn. The canal's rapid success prompted the growth of a new town, along with a complex of locks, basins and warehouses, workers' housing and even an hotel. Much of this is still there, now devoted to pleasure boats of all kinds, and reflecting, in a rather battered and faded way, the elegance of 18th-century classicism. At the centre is a clock

tower, standing guard over a lively and colourful scene. One of the most enjoyable of Britain's canal towns, Stourport sets the tone for the canal as a whole, which quickly assumes its distinctive rural and traditional character.

The next town is Kidderminster, famous for carpets, the Severn Valley Steam Railway, and for Rowland Hill, the founder of the Penny Post, born here in 1793. A statue celebrates his 'creative mind and patient energy', qualities still useful in any dealings with the Post Office. However, the canal's most memorable feature, the cliffs of red sandstone that flank its western side, are already apparent before Kidderminster. This ridge, which the canal follows for 15 miles, turns the route into something tortuous and dramatic. Overhung with all kinds of greenery from the sheer walls, the canal achieves an almost Amazonian quality. Missing only are the parrots. Cut into the red rock are short tunnels, locks and even store rooms and an old stable for the towpath horses. Part of this strange geological feature is Kinver Edge, a high ridge that rears up

Above: *A former towing horse stable cut into the sandstone cliff by Debdale lock.*

Right: *A rural mooring at Tixall.*

Opposite: *At Aldersley Junction the Birmingham Canal meets the Staffs & Worcs. Beyond the bridge is the start of the long flight of locks that rises up to Wolverhampton.*

behind the village of Kinver, covered in gorse and heather and offering views towards the Welsh borders.

The Staffs & Worcs is really just a continuous series of delightful scenes, with contributions made by old brick bridges, locks, lock cottages with pretty gardens, the characteristic iron towpath bridges, split in the centre to allow the passage of the horse's towing rope, old wharves, a series of circular weirs, overgrown tunnels, and an unusual range of trees and flowers. Memorable also are the set of three locks at the Bratch, with their octagonal toll house, a setting guaranteed to appear regularly in canal calendars.

The success in commercial terms of the Staffs & Worcs was greatly helped by the other canals that join it. The Stourbridge Canal, a direct link to the industrial heart of Birmingham and the Black Country which opened throughout in 1792, starts its heavily locked climb towards Dudley at Stourton Junction, near where 18th-century Stourton Castle (a private home) can be seen across the river,

birthplace in 1500 of Cardinal Pole, Mary Tudor's Archbishop of Canterbury. Partly derelict by the early 1960s, the Stourbridge Canal was restored and reopened 25 years ago. Even more significant in trade terms were the junctions at Aldersley with the Birmingham Canal and Autherley with the Birmingham & Liverpool, later the Shropshire Union Canal. As these junctions, effectively a crossing of the Staffs & Worcs, were half a mile apart, traffic using these new rival routes was forced to travel this short stretch of Staffs and Worcs water. In order to overcome the serious drop in revenue that these rivals, with their more direct routes represented, the Staffs & Worcs charged exorbitant tolls for the use of its canal, and for some years this half mile of canal generated most of its income. In the days of cutthroat rivalry between canal companies, such behaviour was not unusual.

Blending as it does so well with its setting, the Staffs & Worcs would not look out of place in some late 18th-century landscape painting. It is full of picturesque elements, even in its northern section,

Above: *Early morning at Tixall lock.*

where it crosses a flatter and more predictable stretch of countryside. Still there are pretty villages, despite the continual proximity of industry lurking over the eastern horizon. As it happens, the best country house on the route is not 18th-century at all. Wightwick Manor was built between 1887 and 1893, and it stands overlooking the canal, a splendidly rich vernacular revival house, extravagantly timber-framed and full of Arts and Crafts details. The interior is still largely William Morris, and it is one of the best examples in England of the avant-garde taste of some late Victorian industrialists. By a strange chance, the canal's other great house, or rather the remains of it, is a Tudor building of the kind that inspired the architect of Wightwick Manor. This is the grand gatehouse at Tixall, a powerful monument to the influence of the Renaissance in Britain. In front of it the canal, widened here into a lake, becomes the major component of an ornamental park. Only the brightly coloured hire boats and the fishermen in their shapeless plastic clothes look out of place. It is a theatrical sight, deceptively imposing because it is, after all, a gatehouse, and behind there is not a great mansion, but simply a field of grazing cows.

The canal ends in fine style at Great Haywood, its junction to the Trent & Mersey framed by the most elegant of towpath bridges, a beautifully flattened arch of soft red brick. Here, late 18th-century boatmen could turn left towards Liverpool and the Mersey, or right towards the Trent and the other canal connections that led ultimately to the Thames, experiencing the reality of Brindley's dream of linking the four great rivers of England. Today, the choice is still there, along with most of the canal routes that had been opened by the end of the 18th century, but few modern boaters, speeding on their way, spare much of a thought for either the age of the system they are using, or the revolution it represented in commercial terms. To travel from here to London takes about five days, five days of long hours of slow cruising interspersed with short bursts of sweat, tears and, occasionally, blood. With the same journey taking two hours by train, it is easy to see why the canal age in Britain was relatively short. Yet, for the early canal boatman, the ability to travel all the way to London was little short of a miracle.

Opposite: *Sunset at Great Haywood, the northern end of the Staffs & Worcs.*

PLACES TO VISIT

Hartlebury Castle, 2 miles E of Stourport: moated, pink sandstone mansion, 15th-century, gothicised in 1750, seat of the Bishops of Worcester; its north wing houses the Hereford & Worcester County Museum.

Kidderminster: Severn Valley Railway, runs 16 miles along scenic river valley to Bewdley and Bridgnorth; large collection of locos etc.

Kinver Edge: a wood and heath-covered sandstone ridge; cave dwellings at Holy Austin Rock inhabited until the 1950s (one now restored); start of the Staffordshire Way, waymarked long-distance path through Cannock Chase, Churnet Valley and Congleton Edge to Mow Cop.

Moseley Old Hall, Fordhouses: Elizabethan house, hiding place of Charles II after Battle of Worcester; 17th-century box parterre garden planted solely with 17th-century plants.

Shugborough Hall, near Great Haywood Junction: Lichfield family seat being restored by the National Trust as a 19th-century working estate; servants' quarters re-created in the stable block, Georgian farmstead housing working farm museum, parkland, rose gardens, etc.

West Midland Safari and Leisure Park, 2 miles W of Kidderminster on A456: drive-around wild animal safari park; variety of rides in the Leisure Park.

Wightwick Manor, 4 miles W of Wolverhampton, accessible on foot from canal from Wightwick Bridge: remarkable Arts & Crafts house, begun 1887; William Morris wallpapers and fabrics, Kempe glass, de Morgan tiles, pre-Raphaelite paintings, Victorian/Edwardian garden (National Trust).

Wolverley: Lock Inn, famous canal pub with terrace alongside lock.

The Cromford Canal

*I*N THE 1770S and 1780s Britain was gripped by canal mania, with speculators desperate to invest their money in the most unlikely schemes. Many of these inevitably came to nothing, but a good number of the waterways that exist today can trace their origins back to this period. It was a time when many practical men allowed their heads to be turned by intemperate enthusiasm, and many decisions were made, not on grounds of sound business practice and common sense, but from the fear of being left behind in the mad rush to plan canals all over the face of Britain. Some of the wilder schemes were never even started or were abandoned when partially completed, others that were finished proved to be total commercial failures, and even the more successful often fell upon hard times from the late 19th century onwards. The number of canals remaining open to traffic has been declining steadily. Many of those that were closed were subsequently obliterated, either by railway lines or by later redevelopment, but others survived, albeit in a derelict state, the visible legacy of that period of frenetic waterway activity.

Two centuries later, in the 1970s, canal mania reared its head again, but the schemes that seized the minds of enthusiasts this time were concerned not with creating new canals, but with restoring the ones that had been closed years before. Fired by the success of a number of major restoration projects, such as the Kennet & Avon, Brecon & Abergavenny and Stratford-on-Avon canals, and the River Avon Navigation – projects that had pioneered the principle of the volunteer workforce – enthusiasts began to consider every closed canal in restoration terms. Gripped by a fervour that made them almost

The derelict and overgrown canal approaching Butterley tunnel.

The Cromford Canal

From the Erewash Canal at Langley Mill, in Nottinghamshire, to Cromford, in Derbyshire 14½ miles long, with 14 broad locks
Short branch from Ironville to Pinxton, 2¼ miles long
Largely closed 50 years ago and partially obliterated since, the Cromford survives in recognisable form only between Ambergate and Cromford, a 5-mile section that has been fully restored.

Notable features Great Northern Basin at Langley Mill, Butterley tunnel, the Pinxton branch at Ironville, Wigwell aqueduct over the River Derwent, Leawood steam pump, Cromford basin and Arkwright Mills, the route of the Cromford and High peak Railway.

History First proposed in 1787, the Cromford Canal was conceived as a valuable extension northwards from Langley Mill, the terminus of the Erewash Canal, to provide an outlet for the coal mines and stone quarries adjacent to the Derwent Valley. The route was surveyed by William Jessop and he was appointed engineer, with Benjamin Outram and Thomas Dadford as his assistants. Construction began in 1789 and the canal was opened throughout in 1794. Supported largely by local industrialists and businessmen, the Cromford was quickly successful. Coal was, as anticipated, the primary cargo, but the canal also served local stone quarries, lead works and the textile mills of Sir Richard Arkwright, as well as carrying agricultural produce and other local materials. A series of tramways was built between the canal and outlying coal mines and quarries. In 1831 the Cromford and High Peak Railway was opened, linking the Cromford with the Peak Forest Canal at Whaley Bridge, and thus opening a direct route to Manchester. The 1830 to 1850 period was the most successful and profitable for the canal's shareholders, with annual tonnage topping 320,000. Always fearful of railway competition, the canal's directors sold the whole enterprise in 1852 to the grandly named Manchester, Buxton, Matlock and Midlands Junction Railway, which later passed into the ownership of the Midland Railway. This marked the start of a gradual decline that continued through the late 19th century. There were problems of subsidence with the long Butterley tunnel, which collapsed in 1889, was

repaired and then collapsed again in 1900. This cut the canal into two and, although some local trade continued, it was the beginning of the end. Disused by the 1930s, the Cromford was largely closed in 1944. Much of the route south of Butterley has subsequently been obliterated, but the isolated stretch from Ambergate north to Cromford has gradually been restored.

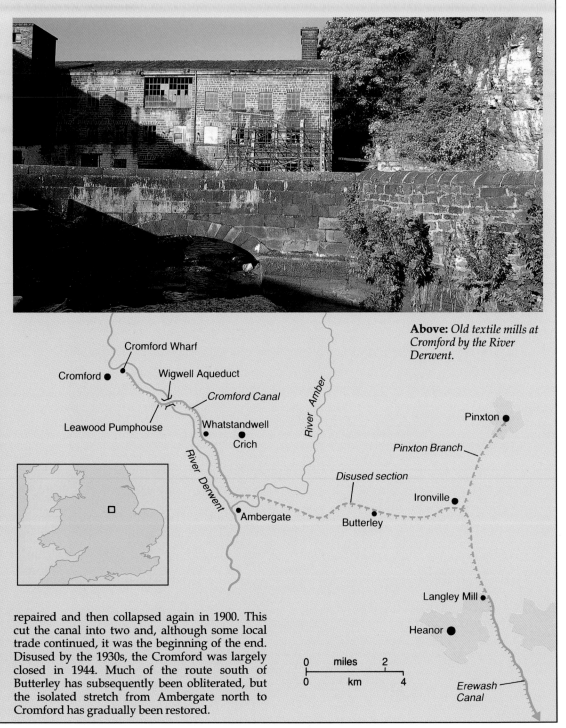

Above: *Old textile mills at Cromford by the River Derwent.*

as blind to reality as their ancestors had been two centuries before, they set up restoration projects all over Britain. Money was raised and work started on a whole range of schemes, often without due consideration being given to their viability or to the environmental questions raised by restoration. It is clear that the reopening of certain canals can be beneficial, both to their locality and to the national network as a whole. It is equally clear, however, that elsewhere the arguments against restoration can be pretty strong.

A long-closed canal is often attractive because of the very nature of its dereliction. To find a broken and overgrown lock chamber hidden in the woods, or a crumbling bridge that crosses a reed-filled ditch in the middle of a field, is exciting because of the picturesque nature of the decay and for the vision of history offered by such forgotten artefacts. The technique of establishing patterns of history from the evidence on the ground is enjoyable and demanding, and brings together archaeology and conjecture in a way that often is no longer seen as useful. When cleaned up and repaired, such things lose a major part of their appeal. There is also the danger that they then become little more than components in the great nostalgia theme park that is being spread, year by year, over the face of Britain, their particular quality violated for ever by the all-powerful concept of Heritage. The pleasures of exploring a derelict canal were all to do with the challenge of finding its remains on the ground, of turning marks on a map into visible reality. The sense of achievement was in direct proportion to the difficulties of the route. Following a level and well-marked trail, with all the problems of access and trespass overcome, and with every structure neatly repaired and adorned with information panels, is all very well, but it is an approach that does little to allow for a spirit of adventure. It also highlights the rival demands of conflicting interests. Those who want to restore canals wish to bring them back, understandably, to a full navigational state. However, the impact of motor-powered boats

on an environment that has been completely wild and undeveloped for decades can be extremely damaging. Even the bicycle wheel and the walker's boot may destroy exactly that quality of nature that their owners have come to admire. What is required is, as always, a sense of balance, a realisation that some derelict canals could, and should, be restored, while others are far better left well alone. This would also mean that the limited funds of money available could be concentrated on the major projects, instead of being scattered, like grapeshot, all over the place.

Among the canals which became candidates for restoration during the 1970s are the Thames & Severn, from Lechlade to Stroud, the Montgomery branch of the Llangollen from Frankton to Newtown, the two trans-Pennine rivals, the Rochdale and the Huddersfield Narrow, the Wey & Arun, the Basingstoke and, in Scotland, the Forth & Clyde, along with a whole scattering of lesser

Above: *The overgrown course of the canal near Ironville.*

Above: *The battered stone bridge that marks the junction with the former Pinxton branch at Ironville.*

Opposite: *The eastern portal of Butterley tunnel.*

would extend this to Cromford, with a branch to Pinxton. After some discussion this, the Cromford Canal, was authorised by Parliament early in 1789. William Jessop was appointed engineer with, as his assistants, Benjamin Outram and Thomas Dadford, and so this short and relatively straightforward waterway was certainly well equipped with engineering talent. Jessop and Outram built many of the East Midlands canals, while Dadford is best known for his work in Wales and the West Midlands. From the start the Cromford had plenty of local supporters, notably among the industrialists who owned or operated the coal mines, stone quarries, iron and lead works and textile mills that were along or near to the proposed route. A major figure was Sir Richard Arkwright, a powerful but enlightened industrialist whose not entirely altruistic support for the Cromford was akin to that of his friend Josiah Wedgwood for the Trent & Mersey. A measure of the local support for the canal is the ease with which the money for its construction was raised. When Jessop presented his estimate, some £42,700, half was raised the same day, and the rest within a fortnight. In the event, when it opened in August 1794, it had cost nearly £79,000. It is remarkable how even the most experienced and honourable of engineers, then as now, were incapable of preparing an accurate cost estimate. As it turned out, this was not a disaster, for the Cromford quickly established its place in the market, and the shareholders were well satisfied with their returns. At its peak in the early 1840s the canal was carrying over 320,000 tons per year.

It was not a very long canal, a little over 14½ miles from end to end, but its route up the Amber and Derwent valleys was quite demanding in engineering terms. There were 14 broad locks, from Langley Mill to Butterley, where the canal company had to build a long tunnel. This tunnel, at 3,063yds the third longest in Britain at the time of its opening, was built to a narrow gauge to save money, and constantly caused problems. Traffic was delayed by the time it took to leg the boats

waterways where partial restoration was only ever a possibility. These range from the Grand Western in Devon to the northern part of the Lancaster Canal. Some of these schemes will be completed in due course, while others will never get beyond the fertile imagination of their supporters who will have to content themselves with a bit of towpath clearing or some patching up of isolated locks and bridges. And others should never have been started at all.

One of the best examples of a long-closed waterway that combines both practical, and valuable, restoration with complete dereliction is the Cromford Canal. Conceived in the late 1780s, the Cromford was one of a number of waterways in the East Midlands inspired by the commercial success of the River Trent and the Trent & Mersey Canal. In 1779 a short canal had been opened to run northwards from the Trent for 12 miles to Langley Mill. Ten years later a scheme was proposed that

through, boatmen hated it because it was so narrow and daunting, and it suffered from subsidence caused by local coal mines. It collapsed in 1889 and was not reopened until 1893, having cost over £7,000 to repair, and then it collapsed again in 1900. This time it was closed for good, cutting the canal in half. Collapsing or subsiding tunnels frequently caused canals to be closed, major examples being Sapperton on the Thames & Severn, Greywell on the Basingstoke and the nightmarish 3,795yd-long Lappal on the Dudley Extension, which took four hours to leg through. Although impassable, and completely unrestorable, many of these tunnels remain as impressive monuments to the extraordinary dynamism of 18th-century canal builders. Looking into the mouth of a long-closed tunnel certainly gets the imagination going, and Butterley is a strong contender in the field. It is, in any case, a name of great significance in 19th-century history, for it was iron from the Butterley furnaces that built the great train shed at St Pancras, and many other structures of the railway age. The name lives on, for Butterley is today the home of the Midland Railway Centre, a major steam museum and operating preserved railway. Closed tunnels can, of course, have other claims to fame. Greywell, near Basingstoke, is known throughout the world for its colony of 2,000 bats, a classic case where restoration, even if practical, would be completely destructive in environmental terms.

The Cromford's other major features were its two aqueducts, both of which suffered partial collapse while being built and were repaired at Jessop's own expense, one costing him twice his annual salary. The smaller of the two carried the canal over the Amber, but was demolished in 1968. Luckily the much more impressive Wigwell aqueduct, which takes the canal over the Derwent in one mighty 80ft single span masonry arch, is still standing, showing

Left: *Near Leawood an iron aqueduct carries the canal over the railway line.*

no signs of the problems it caused Jessop. Another recurring problem for the canals of the East Midlands, but not the Cromford in particular, was flooding. Canals based on river navigations, or running alongside large rivers, can be rendered impassable for long periods by sudden rises in water levels. I have seen the Soar flooded north of Leicester, to the point where the changes in level achieved by the locks disappeared beneath a huge expanse of water. Another time, travelling south along the Oxford Canal, I came to the point near Bletchingdon where the canal joins the River Cherwell, to find that the flooding river had completely filled the fields, leaving no sign of the canal's course. As it left the lock, the boat was snatched by the fast-flowing current and borne at great speed into what seemed to be a huge inland lake. Luckily, I knew the canal well and, following normal twists and turns by keeping a set distance from the top of the towpath hedge, I came safely to the next lock. Had I gone straight on, as seemed possible, I would have finished up firmly aground, in a state of high embarrassment, in the middle of a field a long way from the canal, and surrounded by sheep when the waters subsided, as they did a day or two later.

Coal was the Cromford's main cargo, but equally important were stone, iron and textiles. Quarries and mines not directly on the canal's route were connected to it by tramways, one of the most important of which ran from Ambergate to the great limestone quarry at Crich, now, rather incongruously, the home of the Tramway Museum. There were also passenger services. In 1797 a twice weekly service was started between Nottingham and Cromford at a cost of 5s First Class and 3s Second. Trade was encouraged by the gradual expansion of the Trent network. The Nottingham Canal was opened to Langley Mill in 1796, and from the Erewash there was a canal to Derby. Much of the traffic was local, but long distance carrying was encouraged by the opening, to the Trent, of the Leicester line of the Grand Junction. Even more

Above: In the early days of the canal, coal was its staple cargo.

Below: Old sign on a warehouse at High Peak Junction, where the Cromford & High Peak Railway met the Cromford Canal.

important was the start, in 1831, of the extraordinary Cromford & High Peak Railway which, with its inclines and winding engines, spanned the gap between Cromford and Whaley Bridge on the Peak Forest Canal, and opened up a through route to Manchester. For years one of the most interesting sights of the Cromford must have been the complex and continuous process of transhipment between the boats at the wharves and the wagons of railways, and the hauling of the wagons up and down the steep incline, whose course across the hillside is easy to follow. This route across the Peaks had been first proposed as a canal, but the difficulties of the landscape made a railway a far more practical answer. The Cromford Canal always had close railway connections and it passed quite early into railway ownership. In 1852 the directors sold it as a going concern for £103,500 to the promoters of the Manchester, Buxton, Matlock & Midlands Junction Railway, and in due course it became part of the giant Midland Railway. From this point, trade steadily declined, with the canal suffering more and more from the Midland

and Great Northern Railway lines that duplicated much of its route. By 1888 trade had dropped to just under 46,000 tons per year and the final collapse of Butterley tunnel in 1900 brought the canal to its knees. Some local trade continued, particularly on the southern section and then, after years of quiet decay, it was progressively closed between 1944 and 1962. Some sections were obliterated, while others were just abandoned and left to their own devices.

With the great revival of interest in canals and other visible relics of industrialisation that occurred from the late 1960s onwards, the Cromford came slowly back into the limelight. It was an ideal waterway for both the casual canal enthusiast and the serious student of the new discipline of industrial archaeology. Along its length were to be found steam pumps and the old wharves, bridges and aqueducts, tunnels, basins and much else besides. Along its banks were the remains of the great industries that had inspired it, the textile mills, coal mines, iron furnaces, quarries, lime kilns and lead works, along with their network of railways. In the early 1960s a good deal of this was still there, but much else was swept away during that decade of national destruction. My first visit was in the late 1960s when I came to look at Arkwright's great cotton mill, a grand stone block still straddling the Derwent Valley as it did in Joseph Wright's gloomy late 18th-century painting. The canal basin and its old warehouses were nearby, overgrown and uncared for, together with the remaining bits of the High Peak Railway. After many years of restoration and tidying up things are different now. Then, a short walk took me past the Leawood Pump House, across Jessop's fine aqueduct and along the towpath to the portal of the short Gregory tunnel. The rest of the route southwards I explored by car, driving first along the steeply wooded Derwent Valley, and enjoying the tight proximity of road, river, canal and railway, forced together by the nature of the landscape. It was necessary to stop the car from time to time to

go and find the canal, for it was rarely visible from the road, and this was not without its difficulties. The hurtling lorries on the A6 seemed particularly intolerant of a car whose driver was reading a map and thinking about canals. I survived, and found that as far as Ambergate the canal was still there, and in quite good condition. I am grateful to those early years of waterway exploration, for they taught me much about reading the landscape, not to mention the particular technique of following a highly detailed Ordnance Survey map, looking out of the window and driving the car, all at the same time and without doing mischief to myself or to others, a very necessary skill for anyone in the guide book business. I have friends who have taken this to a higher plane by additionally eating sandwiches and drinking a cup of coffee, all at the same time, but I have not followed in their footsteps, preferring to have an excuse to stop the car from time to time.

From Ambergate I was more dependent upon the map, for sections of the canal had disappeared

Above: *The stern of an old wooden barge at Cromford wharf.*

Opposite: *The classical splendour of Leawood pump house, housing a steam pump installed to lift water from the Derwent to feed the canal.*

Above: *Remains of a lock chamber near Ironville.*

industry. Presumably the finished china was sent to market by canal boat, carefully packed in straw-filled barrels that would make their laborious way to a smart retailer in London, carried down the Cromford and the Erewash, on to the Trent, and then south via the Trent & Mersey, the Coventry and the Oxford canals to the Thames, or down the Leicester line to the Grand Junction, and thus to London. It is a vision of another world, and one that has gone for ever. The whole route still exists, except for the Cromford bit, but to travel it again by boat does not really tell you much. It is a different experience today, simply because it does not have to be done. Canal travel is for pleasure, in one's own time, and so no one can in any way even imagine the lives of all those boatmen, lock keepers and others whose existence was entirely taken up by the need to get that barrel of Pinxton porcelain to London. From Ironville the main line of the canal turns south, but there was then, and is now, precious little to be seen. Obliteration has been very thorough and all the locks have gone. Only the names of pubs such as The Boat Inn give any clue to the canal's former existence. The Cromford ended at the Great Northern Basin at Langley Mill, in its time a major interchange centre and meeting ground for boats and their cargoes coming from Cromford, Nottingham, Derby and the Trent. Today, much restored and cleaned up, the Basin is a satisfactory terminus for the Erewash Canal, once the northern limit of the Grand Union's empire.

Since my first visit, I have been back to the Cromford several times, more attentive now to the canal which has been the subject of a long restoration project. The isolated 5-mile section from Cromford south towards Ambergate is fully restored. The Leawood steam pump is back in business, its massive beam engine again raising water 30ft from the Derwent to feed the canal, and the whole towpath has been turned into a very pleasant walk. Restoration may have swept away the more picturesque aspects of the Cromford in decay, but it does make it more accessible, and thus

completely. Its route turned eastwards, to follow the River Amber, and I was just in time to see the Ball Bridge aqueduct that took the canal over the river, shortly before its demolition. I also made my way by lanes and tracks to both portals of Butterley tunnel. The western portal is the more impressive architecturally, a hefty structure enlarged at a later date to carry a railway across the tunnel mouth, but the eastern one is far more emotive, a little hole in a steep hillside, seemingly too small for the boats that had to pass through it. One can still sense the lowering of the spirits it must have provoked at the thought of the hours ahead of legging the boat through the claustrophobic blackness. At Ironville, a town well named in this setting and carrying with it the echo of the relentless demands that Victorian industry made upon its work-force, it was easy to explore the remains of the canal and the junction with the 2¼-mile branch north to Pinxton. Coal was the reason for its building, but I drove up to Pinxton thinking rather of the short-lived porcelain factory set up here in the mid-1790s, and of William Billingsley painting his delicate creamy roses surrounded by the debris and dirt of heavy easier to understand in the context of the industrial history of the region. For some years it was possible to be carried along the restored section of the canal in a horse-drawn narrow boat, an activity not uncommon on various British canals that presents a highly selective view of the history of the waterways. Today, a walk along the very tidy towpath of a fully restored but completely unused and isolated part of the English canal system, complete with captive traditional narrow boats that cannot go anywhere, places the Cromford firmly in the fantasy world projected by the nearby steam railway centre and tramway museum. The real story of the canal, in both economic and social terms, is certainly much harder to present in an acceptable manner to an audience conditioned to see history as a theme park experience. What remains in question is whether this kind of presentation actually makes any sense at all. What is lost for ever is the pleasure of tracking a long-disused canal across the hidden corners of an unfamiliar landscape, using only the clues offered by the map and a reading of the terrain. The realities of such a search are mud and thorn bushes and getting lost, and the physical demands of a landscape that has not been sanitised out of

existence. There is an excitement in wilderness and nature out of control, but the inexorable march of the restorers, the improvers and the manipulators of history seem set to remove all such places from the face of Britain. It is a pity, and I am glad I am old enough to have seen derelict and abandoned canals when no one really cared about them at all.

Above: *Old warehouses at Cromford wharf, the end of the canal.*

PLACES TO VISIT

American Adventure Theme Park, 2 miles SW of Langley Mill: ride the Niagara Rapids or the Cherokee Falls log flume, watch a shoot-out in Silver City, ride a Mississippi paddle steamer, and more.

Cromford Mill: under restoration by the Arkwright Society, guided tours available; shops, craft units, restaurant.

Eastwood: D H Lawrence Birthplace Museum, in the former mining village that was a lifetime influence on the writer.

High Peak Junction: restored railway and canal buildings at the junction of the Cromford & High Peak Railway and the Cromford Canal; towpath walks.

Start of the **High Peak Trail**, a footpath and cycleway which runs 17½ miles west through Black Rock, past Middleton Top Engine House

(see right) and on into the Peak National Park.

Matlock: Riber Castle Wildlife Park, hilltop site for rare animals park, dominated by the ruins of a fairy-tale mid-19th-century folly.

Matlock Bath: Gulliver's Kingdom Theme Park, rides for 5–12 year olds.

Heights of Abraham, cable cars climb to the country park at the summit; two show caverns, nature trail, superb views.

Peak District Mining Museum, illustrates Derbyshire's lead industry from Roman times to the present.

Temple Mine, restored 1920s and 1930s lead and fluorspar workings.

Midland Railway Centre, Butterley, 1 mile N of Ripley: steam trains run 3½ miles between Butterley Station and Riddings; Midland Railway exhibits, locos and rolling stock.

National Tramway Museum, Crich: collection of

vintage tramcars some of which offer rides (with views over Derwent Valley); reconstructed period street.

Nottingham: highlights include the castle, the 15th-century Church of St Mary's, the Gothic Revival Roman Catholic cathedral, the Canal Museum, the Lace Hall's story of Nottingham lace, the Tales of Robin Hood, and a number of other museums.

Wirksworth: Heritage Centre has displays on lead mining and explains the local custom of well dressings (which may be seen during the Spring Bank Holiday).

Middleton Top Engine House, 1½ miles NW, houses the beam engine built in 1829 for the Cromford & High Peak Railway to haul wagons up from the Middleton limestone mine.

National Stone Centre, the story of stone, set in an old quarry.

The Canals of North Staffordshire and Cheshire

MANY YEARS ago I lived for a time beside the Trent and Mersey Canal. It was on the border between Staffordshire and Cheshire, at a place called Red Bull, after the local pub. Nearby, the Macclesfield Canal branched away on its lovely rural route northwards. From the house, one of a tight terrace of four known as Pickford Cottages and built originally to house employees of the canal carrying company whose name is now linked firmly with road transport, it was possible to see the start of the great flight of locks that took the Trent & Mersey Canal down to Middlewich and the Cheshire Plain. I often walked down beside these locks, 29 in all, many of them side by side in pairs, quiet now as the canal wound its way among the trees but still bearing the scars of heavy and continuous traffic of years ago. I thought often of all those canal families working their laborious and exhausting way up what, for good reason, was popularly known as Heartbreak Hill. It was the women and children who worked the locks, and the images of them struggling in wind and rain, familiar to me from 19th-century engravings, came to life all too easily in the mind.

Walking the other way along the Trent & Mersey, I would come quickly to Kidsgrove and thus to the mouth of the Harecastle tunnel, a gloomy and uninviting hole surrounded by water always stained dramatically red. To the side, overgrown and unbelievably small, lay the entrance to James Brindley's original tunnel, long closed due to

Emerging from the northern end of the Harecastle tunnel, with the waters of the Trent & Mersey stained red by iron.

The Macclesfield Canal

From Hardings Wood Junction on the Trent and Mersey Canal near Kidsgrove to Marple Junction on the Peak Forest Canal
28 miles long, with 13 narrow locks
Notable features Embankments and aqueducts, remote and rural route, Bosley flight of locks, fine stone-built bridges especially the roving or towpath variety, old mills, landscape and Peak views.

Peak Forest Canal

Marple
Marple Junction
High Lane
Higher Poynton
Bollington
Macclesfield

0   miles   5
0   km   10

Macclesfield Canal

Congleton

Kent Green   Mow Cop
Kidsgrove   Hardings Wood Junction
Trent & Mersey Canal

History There were a number of schemes for canals to link the Midlands and Manchester from the 1770s but it was not until 1825 that Thomas Telford surveyed and selected the route that the canal was actually to follow. When construction started Telford had moved on to other things and so the work was supervised by another engineer, William Crosley. However, the finished canal, which was opened in 1831, bore all the Telford hallmarks. Despite its late completion, the canal was successful, offering as it did a direct and quick link between the Midlands and Manchester for cargoes of coal, cotton, stone, pottery materials and so on. In 1846 the Macclesfield, along with the Peak Forest and Ashton canals, was bought by a railway company, and through amalgamations they ended up in the ownerhip of the Great Central Railway. Despite this, the pattern of successful trade continued until the early part of this century, when increasing competition from rail and road brought about a rapid decline in the canal's fortunes. The Macclesfield shared the fate of most other narrow canals in Britain but, although commercial traffic had completely disappeared by the 1960s, it was never actually closed. It was thus able to benefit from the upsurge in pleasure boating that began in the late 1960s, even though its northern links to Manchester were by then closed. Since the reopening of the Peak Forest and Ashton links, it has become an important part of the Cheshire Ring of cruising waterways.

Right: *The old flour mill near Macclesfield, a typical industrial building of the area.*

subsidence caused by local mining. Opened in 1777 after 11 years of digging, this great endeavour was, rightly, seen as one of the wonders of the world. I could never see it without thinking about the intrepid 'navigators', or navvies, who spent years of their lives working away deep underground in the dark, the wet and the filth, using nothing but shovels, to create this tunnel 1¾ miles long through the rock and the clay. And then there were the generations of canal boatmen who, until the early years of this century, had to spend long and wearisome hours legging their heavy craft through the dripping darkness.

Lying awake at night, I heard sometimes the clanking rattle of the iron lock paddles rising and falling as some boat made its nocturnal way through the locks. Always I wanted to know where they had come from, and where they were going to, and I wanted above all else to make similar journeys myself, a private passage through a sleeping landscape.

The house was well placed for explorations of the local canals, and so soon I came to know the Macclesfield, the Peak Forest, the Trent & Mersey and the Caldon quite well. It seemed a varied yet self-contained little group of waterways within a far greater network whose tentacles spread far beyond my limited horizons. At first, visits were by car or on foot, and thus isolated and fragmentary, but in due course I was able to travel all these routes by boat, and thus develop the intimacy with the canals and their landscape that is accessible only to those who travel in this manner. Even Heartbreak Hill in the wind and rain soon held no real terrors, tiredness kept easily in check by the anticipated satisfaction of reaching the top lock, and by the certain knowledge that I did not have to do it. Pleasure boating is exactly that, and you can stop when you want, unimpeded by the pressures of timetables and the need to earn a living.

Left: *Travelling south down the Bosley locks on the Macclesfield Canal.*

Opposite: *The Red Bull aqueduct carries the Macclesfield Canal high above the Trent & Mersey.*

The Macclesfield Canal

It was the Macclesfield Canal that I first knew well, attracted by the efficiency and grandeur of the engineering of what was, in relative terms, a very late canal. Its opening in 1831, well into the railway age, should have doomed it to a slow and lingering death, the hopes of its promoters never to be fulfilled, and its shareholders never to be repaid. That was the fate of so many 18th-century canals, let alone those built in the 19th century. Yet the Macclesfield was, against the run of things, a great success, and it prospered for many years. The key was the quick and direct route it offered between the north Midlands and Manchester, a route carefully planned by one of the greatest of the canal engineers, Thomas Telford. The hand, and mind, of Telford are still easily discerned, notably in the route along the side of a ridge of hills and set at the most efficient contour level, in the grouping of the canal's locks into a single flight, at Bosley, in the quality and scale of the bridges and structures, in the large reservoirs ensuring a plentiful water supply for the canal even in summer and, above all else, in the tremendous cutting and the towering embankments that maintain the canal's chosen level. These are the hallmarks of this great engineer, and they help to make the canal a distinctive feature in an already impressive landscape. They also helped to ensure that coal, cotton and much else besides continued to be carried along the Macclesfield Canal well into this century. It was the lorry, and not the train, that finally killed off its trade.

The Macclesfield was, therefore, for many decades a busy and successful commercial waterway and so its rural nature today comes as something of a surprise, its remoteness remarkable in what is a well-populated, and popular, stretch of the countryside. The sense of isolation is a legacy of the time when the Macclesfield was little more than a long rural cul de sac, its northern end cut off from the rest of the network by the closure of the Ashton Canal from the 1960s. This was the vital link to Manchester and without it the canal became a 28-mile backwater, interesting to only two of the many kinds of pleasure boaters, those who want to potter about and go nowhere very far, and those who want to visit every canal in the network. The former have always existed in large numbers but the latter are an increasingly rare species. It was the former group who kept the Macclesfield alive during its period of isolation, a period coinciding with a time when large-scale closures throughout the canal network seemed all too likely. Cruising clubs and hire bases were set up, and traffic flowed along the Macclesfield, particularly at weekends. It was enough to keep the waters moving, and the canal in business. Eventually the tide of opinion turned and canals came back into favour, in their new guise as leisure amenities. Thanks to its geographical position at the heart of Manchester's southern suburbs, the Macclesfield was bound to be high on anyone's amenity list, and so its future was quickly assured. It took some time, but eventually the authorities began to realise that boats are boats whether they are carrying coal or people, and that pleasure boating generates as much use as commercial traffic, if not more. From the 1970s restoration took over from closure as the favoured option and, with the reopening of the Ashton Canal, the Macclesfield once again became part of a through route. Today, as a vital part of the so-called Cheshire Ring, a 97-mile touring circuit designed to take up comfortably the two weeks that is the average canal holiday, the Macclesfield Canal is probably busier than it has been since the last century.

Hardings Wood Junction is the start of the Macclesfield, and it leaves the Trent & Mersey Canal in a rather curious manner. The branch actually runs to the south, contrary to what you expect. The two canals are then side by side for a while, until the Macclesfield turns to the north to cross the Trent & Mersey, whose locks have now taken it to a lower level, on an aqueduct. It is exactly the sort of junction favoured by road

engineers today, and demonstrates what foresight Telford had. The canal is then carried over a road on a second big aqueduct before plunging into a deep cutting which successfully hides it from the surrounding suburbia. Another curiosity here is the stop lock. With its short fall of only 1ft, this was designed simply to keep the water belonging to the Trent & Mersey Company from flowing into the territory of the Macclesfield Canal Company. It was also a convenient place for the collecting of tolls in the days of commercial carrying. Emerging from the cutting, the canal takes its place in the landscape, its handsome stone bridges, beautifully proportioned and detailed, reflecting the care taken by its designers and builders. Here also is the first of the swing bridges, balanced structures made immensely heavy by disuse in the days of the canal's decline. It was beside one of these that there used to be the kind of canalside pub that today exists only in dreams, and films. Little more than a house, its bar was a front room with tables served by the landlady who collected the drinks from her

cellar, the beer being delivered in a jug. Remote, informal and delightfully impractical, it was a rare survival from another age, and as out of place as the coal boats it used to serve. The landlady died a few years ago and the old pub is now a private house.

The best feature of the Macclesfield is probably its landscape, and the views its route continuously offers. To the east is a line of hills, summits crowned first by the gothic folly known as Mow Cop Castle and then by the distinctive rounded hilltop of The Cloud, reminders that the Pennines are never very far away. To the west, the land falls gently away towards the far views across the Cheshire Plain. This is a particularly English landscape, green and lush, and the canal adds the essential element of water, the reflective foreground so favoured by 18th-century painters. At Ramsdell Hall the painting comes to life, a classical 18th-century mansion set in parkland against a distant view of hills, facing out over a landscape that is initially composed, and then increasingly natural. Lawns run down to the canal, which forms the boundary between the formal and informal. It is Blenheim on a small scale, with the canal the essential water feature, its towpath lined by elegant cast iron fencing. Today it is a scene of English perfection, but what did the owners of the Hall think when the riotous navvies came to build the canal through their park?

When I was last on this stretch, there was a brightly painted traveller's boat around the next corner, out of sight of the Hall. Its roof was covered with various crops growing in tubs; a goat was attacking the towpath hedge. Every now and then the goat jumped delicately on to the boat, walked carefully along the catwalk beside the cabin and stretched up towards the tubs on the roof. Held by its rope, it could never quite reach, and so, turning precisely, it jumped back on to the towpath. Living on a canal boat is, for many, the perfect escape. So long as you keep moving in a desultory fashion, you are left alone. In principle a boat can stay in any one place for a fortnight but with 2,000 miles of

Below: *Unusual crew members on a narrow boat near Ramsdell on the Macclesfield Canal.*

waterways in Britain, and much of that remote, such rules are difficult to enforce. All you need is a British Waterways licence and a desire for a wandering life. Once under way, the temptation just to keep going is often hard to resist. The pace of canal life is a great leveller, throwing into doubt and confusion all concepts of 'normality' and challenging conventional attitudes to work and play. There is ample time to reconsider everything, with contexts changed by the emphasis on the minutiae of the surroundings, the small details of the landscape, the intricacies of passing houses and gardens and the lives they represent, and the chance to watch in full minor events and dramas. In a field near the traveller's boat there was a white horse. It had found a gap in the hedge and had wandered away, not far, but into a wider world. From his house the owner could see what had happened and he walked slowly to the horse, saying nothing, but moving quietly behind it. The horse watched the man and then, giving in, turned and went back into its field through the gap. The man mended the gap and went back to his house. The horse neighed and stamped its foot.

The canals are full of people who are running away. Even those on holiday in a hire cruiser are making an escape of a kind. The real escapees are more obvious out of season. In the winter, when the hire craft and weekend boats are all on their moorings, they are to be seen travelling on, smoke drifting up from their fires, couples, often middle-aged or elderly, making a break from the prisons of their lives, men on their own, in somewhat decrepit boats, fleeing God knows what domestic drama.

Near Astbury, a pretty village with a spectacular church, there is a golf course, with greens on both sides of the canal. Serious golfers cross to and from wearing the extaordinary pullovers favoured only by their kind, wheeling their bags and paying no attention at all to the canal. It is simply an inconvenience, a long watery bunker that must have swallowed thousands of balls for ever. The

canal then skirts round Congleton, keeping away from the town. Here is one of those stone bridges unique to the Macclesfield, a clever answer to the problem posed by the towpath changing sides. An elegant composition of flowing curves, the bridge not only looks good, but also enabled the towing horse to cross the canal without untying the rope from the boat, a fine example of the instinctive

Above: *Golfers at Astbury turning their back on the Macclesfield Canal.*

Below: *A characteristic towpath turnover bridge on the Macclesfield, near Congleton.*

combination of efficiency and visual harmony so characteristic of 19th-century engineers.

The canal crosses the River Dane on an aqueduct and then reaches the Bosley flight of 12 locks, which raises the canal 118ft. It is now over 500ft above sea level, but still overshadowed by the eastern ridge of hills which rises to 1,200ft. One main road crosses the lock flight, but the only way to see the locks properly, and to enjoy their rural seclusion, is on foot or by boat.

As it approaches Macclesfield, the canal swings about, following its contour line, and then takes a discreet easterly route, skirting old suburbs on the hills above the town, and newer industrial estates. The town sits in the valley below, built around the River Bollin, and always in view. Macclesfield is a handsome, dark stone town, ranging over the western slopes of the valley, built on the wealth of the textile trade. A major silk town since the 18th century, Macclesfield has managed to retain both its primary industry and its independence. At the same time, the market place and its interesting range of churches underline its standing since the Middle Ages as an important market town.

The textile trade, or rather the tangible remains of it, dominate the canal route from Macclesfield northwards. A great embankment takes it high above Bollington, with ample time to look down on the old cotton mills. These were the source of the

canal's income, and its success, in the 19th century, and still they stand as gaunt memorials to another age. Bollington is an up-and-down kind of place, all steep hills, embankments and viaducts, and plenty of atmosphere despite the encroaching Manchester suburbs. The Peak National Park is only a mile away, and in any case the hills help to keep the developers at bay. Just to the south, and towering over the canal, is the ridge of Kerridge Hill, crowned by White Nancy, a folly in the form of a sugarloaf-shaped tower of uncertain origin.

Above: *Clarence Mill at Bollington on the Macclesfield Canal.*

Opposite: *Remote Bosley locks and the high embankments of the Macclesfield seen from the summit of The Cloud.*

PLACES TO VISIT

Adlington Hall, 5 miles N of Macclesfield: Tudor timber-framing plus 18th-century brick; grounds include a yew walk and a lime avenue; venue for antiques and craft fairs.

Astbury: St Mary's Church, dates from 1200s, with chunky pillars and good Jacobean painted roof.

Biddulph: Biddulph Grange Garden, rare high Victorian garden restored by National Trust; horticultural world tour through a number of smaller gardens.

Gawsworth Hall, 2½ miles S of Macclesfield: Tudor manor house, birthplace of Mary Fitton, believed to be Shakespeare's 'Dark Lady'; the

tilting ground is thought to be a rare Elizabethan pleasure garden.

Hare Hill, 4 miles NW of Macclesfield: parkland, walled garden (National Trust); link path to Alderley Edge.

Little Moreton Hall, 4 miles SW of Congleton: exceptional example of a 15th-century, timber-framed moated manor house.

Macclesfield: Paradise Mill, former silk mill workers demonstrate silk handloom weaving.

Silk Museum: story of silk told in audio-visuals, tableaux etc.

Marple: see under Peak Forest Canal, page 121.

Mow Cop: Castle, an early (1754) folly, a sham ruin.

Mow Cop Trail: waymarked between Mow Cop and The Cloud, forms first part of Staffordshire Way long-distance footpath; far-reaching views from Congleton Edge.

Nether Alderley Mill, 6 miles W of Macclesfield: overshot tandem wheel watermill, dated to 15th century, restored to full working order (National Trust).

Oakgrove: Fool's Nook Inn, Leek Road, near Sutton, rural canalside pub.

Quarry Bank Mill & Styal Country Park, 1½ miles N of Wilmslow: major cotton mill restored by National Trust as working, water-powered museum of cotton industry. Riverside walks, woodlands.

Manchester is now just a few miles away and yet the canal is more remote than ever. Hidden in the hills, and seen only by minor roads, it follows an intensely private route through a landscape of greens. Even the placenames, far older than the canal, are an echo of the landscape – Whiteley Green, Clark Green, Walkersgreen, Booth Green, Skellorn Green, Wood Lanes, Springbank. It is a strange and secret hinterland, the England that no one really knows but always hopes to find. It is the canals that can often unlock the secrets of that England, quietly making their sinuous way into bits of countryside that are otherwise impenetrable. The boats come through, and pass on, leaving little impression, but taking with them the memory of all these private worlds, an infinite variety of slices of landscape whose isolation is the secret of their survival. Embankments and aqueducts give splendid views out of this private world, glimpses of distant civilisation. One carries the canal over a railway line, near the appropriately named Middlewood Station, itself hidden and seemingly inaccessible. A cutting takes the canal past High Lane, with old mills again underlining its *raison d'être,* and then suddenly it emerges from its isolation into the busy reality of Marple. Here, the Macclesfield ends, joining at a junction and boating centre the older Peak Forest Canal.

The Peak Forest Canal

From Whaley Bridge to Dukinfield Junction on the Ashton Canal
15 miles long, with 16 locks
Notable features Marple flight of locks and Marple aqueduct, Bugsworth Basin and the route of the Doveholes tramway, 1832 transhipment warehouse at Whaley Bridge, hillside route with views over the Goyt Valley, Peak views.
History Authorised by an Act of Parliament in 1794, and planned by Benjamin Outram, the canal was completed in 1800, with the exception of the Marple flight of locks, which took another four years. Built for the limestone trade, the canal was linked at its eastern end to the quarries by a 6½ mile tramway, with Bugsworth Basin becoming a major transhipment centre. Lime and coal were the other staple cargoes, ensuring a long period of prosperity through the 19th century. The canal passed into railway ownership in 1846, but by that time its immediate future had been assured by the opening of both the connecting Macclesfield Canal and the Cromford and High Peak Railway, which ran from Whaley Bridge to the Cromford Canal across the Peaks. By the end of the century the canal was in slow decline. The stone traffic from Bugsworth ceased in the 1920s and by the 1940s through commercial traffic to Manchester via the Marple locks had virtually disappeared. Two serious breaches in the canal embankment near New Mills, in the 1940s and in 1973, further restricted navigation. By the 1960s the western end, from Marple down to the Ashton Canal, was derelict, but in the 1970s both canals were restored and the through route to Manchester was reopened as part of the Cheshire Ring of cruising waterways.

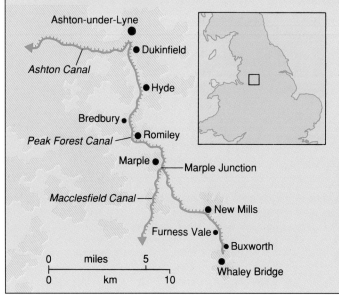

Contrasting styles of canal boat at Marple Junction, where the Macclesfield meets the Peak Forest.

The Peak Forest Canal

The Peak Forest is a very different kind of canal, meandering and small scale, and far more part of the 18th century. It was built in the 1790s for the express purpose of linking the great limestone deposits at Doverholes with the main canal network in Manchester. Planned by the Derbyshire engineer Benjamin Outram, its route ran from the Ashton Canal at Dukinfield, to the east of Manchester, to Whaley Bridge, a Peak village nestling below the limestone ridge. Cut along a contour line high above the Goyt Valley, the canal was a spectacular achievement in its time. There are no locks, the canal making no attempt to climb the extra 1,000ft required to reach the limestone quarries. Instead, the quarries were linked to the canal by tramways, an early example of the successful interaction between canal and railway that was commonplace in the early 19th century. Initially, horse-drawn wagons brought the stone the 6½ miles from Doveholes to a specially built basin at Bugsworth. Here it was either transferred to boats for onward shipment or turned into lime in a great series of coal-fired kilns, lime being the major fertiliser and soil improvement agent continuously in demand by farmers all over Britain. The canal and its associated tramway was in use by 1800, and was immediately successful. The opening of the Macclesfield Canal 30 years later gave it a further boost, as did the completion the same year of the Cromford & High Peak Railway, which provided a direct link to the Cromford Canal on the eastern side of the Peaks.

Whaley Bridge is the best place to start a visit to the Peak Forest Canal. Here, in this hillside village, is the end, or the beginning, of the canal, hidden in a large and handsome stone building, proudly dated 1832. This was the interchange shed for the canal and the Cromford & High Peak Railway, where goods could be transhipped between boats and railway wagons. Originally, railway tracks ran into the shed on either side of the canal, beneath the grand roof that offered protection from the ever-present rain. The Cromford & High Peak was

an extraordinary operation, a series of stretches of railway line linked by steep inclined planes. The wagons were hauled up, or lowered down, these precipitous slopes attached to endless cables powered by stationary engines. Such complex transport arrangements were typical of the 19th century, when imagination and ingenuity was often allowed to triumph over common sense. What is remarkable is that the whole creaking network survived in operation until the 1960s, with clanking steam engines going about their business in the swirling mists and rain of the High Peaks, and wagons rising up and down the inclined planes. Today, it would all be part of some fantasy theme park, but the harsh reality was swept away in that decade of technological change, another Victorian dinosaur made extinct by progress and modern economic theory. Today, the trains and the tracks have gone, but the trackbed survives, along with the slopes of the inclined planes, and these are now

Above: *Whaley Bridge wharf, the terminus of the Peak Forest Canal. In the stone building goods were transhipped between narrow boats and the wagons of the Cromford & High Peak Railway.*

117

all official walkways, a splendid footpath across the Peaks, surrounded by the ghosts of dynamic endeavour and toil.

Whaley Bridge is a small stone town, handsome in a classically English way, devastated by the thundering lorries that are busy taking away the limestone of Derbyshire to bury it under some road or motorway in the far corners of Britain. Anyone standing in the centre of Whaley Bridge for ten minutes could not fail to begin to believe that our continuing infatuation with the motor car and all its work is an act of complete self-destructive lunacy. Despite the noise, life goes on, and Whaley Bridge is a fine vision of a particular Englishness. Two cake shops stand side by side, and across the road is a general store with a big notice in the window offering hemp for sale (for fishing bait, presumably). Other notices advertise the activities of the Buxworth Stripper (pine, that is) and a Boot Fair in aid of the Whaley Bridge Band. The

Mechanics Institute, that centre of Victorian commercial and social fervour, now offers creative music and craft activities. Near the canal basin, in Outram House, is an organisation proudly labelled The Plain English Campaign. Disappointingly, this turns out to be a commercial typesetting and printing business, not some secret revolutionary agency committed to the destruction of red tape and bureaucratic pomposity. Nearby another notice draws attention to *Judith Mary, the Pride of the Peak*. This is a trip boat and restaurant, offering a surprising variety of temptations, including a cream tea cruise (still only £7), a grand buffet, a four-course dinner and a Christmas Special, all while you drift gently along the canal. Best of all though was the Champagne Breakfast, perhaps the most unusual way to start the day in Whaley Bridge.

Leaving Whaley Bridge, the canal sets out on its precipitous hillside journey. First comes the branch leading to Bugsworth Basin, formerly the transhipment centre for the limestone from Doveholes, and then the first of a number of swing bridges. Despite its industrial history, this is a very rural canal, offering intimate views of cottage gardens and grazing horses, domestic details set against a backdrop whose dramatic intensity becomes steadily more apparent. High on its hillside the canal looks out over the Goyt Valley, a blend of exciting landscape and the powerful legacy of industry, dark chimneys and old mills set against the steep and rocky hills. The names echo the Industrial Revolution – Furness Vale and New Mills, towns growing up from the Goyt, the river that originally brought them into being. It is an extraordinary valley, full of the history of industrial England, the river and its mills, then the canal, and finally the three railway lines that run along it, all at different levels. One is beside the canal, one is on the opposite hillside, and the third is near the valley bottom. One result of this is that New Mills, a small, still-industrial stone town that has spread itself across the valley, boasts two railway stations, the

grandly named New Mills Central on the northern crest, and New Mills Newtown on the southern. On a rare sunny day, the valley and its railways take on the look of a complex modern diorama, tiny trains moving through a landscape so condensed with detail that it loses any sense of reality. The canal clings to its precarious hillside perch, making its way to Marple and the junction with the Macclesfield.

From here the Peak Forest carries straight on, plunging immediately into the flight of 16 locks that carries it down towards Manchester, a fall of 210ft. Spread out over a mile, and culminating in the magnificent stone aqueduct that takes the canal high above the Goyt, the Marple flight of locks is simply one of the best canal sights in Britain. The locks, brought back into use not that long ago after years of dereliction and decay, are beautifully sited on the steep hillside, surrounded by woods and parkland that keep the urban sprawl of Marple in its place. The river is far below, hidden by thick woods. Beside the aqueduct an impressive railway viaduct strides across the valley. The Marple locks, a complex and expensive piece of engineering, took years to build and were not completed until 1804, four years after the rest of the canal. During this period, a tramway carried goods across the gap between the two sections of the canal, resulting in complicated and time-consuming transhipping operations between boats and wagons. A direct

Left: An old crane at Whaley Bridge wharf.

response to this was the development of an early form of containerisation, based on iron boxes with a two-ton payload that could more readily be transferred from water to rail and back again. Curiously, this obviously practical solution was not taken up elsewhere until well into the 19th century, by which time it was too late to save the commercial canal network from terminal decline.

Safely across the valley, the canal continues on its still remarkably rural route, making its way past the smart suburb villages of Romiley, Bredbury and Woodley. Two short tunnels add to the interest, and then the canal looks down over the wooded valley of the Tame. Almost with a jolt, it all suddenly changes. The rural idyll comes to an end in the urban muddle of outer Manchester, and the rest of the journey to Dukinfield is unremarkable.

Opposite: The steerer places his boat to enter a lock on the Marple flight without hitting the walls of the bridge, or the lock gates.

PLACES TO VISIT

Buxton: elegant spa town with gracious 18th-century Crescent. Micrarium museum examines wonders of nature through remote-controlled microscopes.

Buxworth: Navigation Inn, by terminus at Bugworth Basin.

Castleton, 10 miles E of Whaley Bridge: heart of Peak National Park. Ruined Peveril Castle. Peak Cavern, walk through tunnels and chambers. Speedwell Cavern, reached only by boat. Treak Cliff Cavern, where translucent Blue John stone is quarried.

Cromford and High Peak Railway (trackbed): access (to walk southwards) near Street House Farm, Pomeroy, on A515, 5 miles SW of Buxton.

Goyt Valley, S of Whaley Bridge: popular beauty spot around Fernilee and Errwood reservoirs with woodland and moorland walks, picnic areas.

Lyme Hall and Park, 1½ miles S of Disley: Elizabethan mansion behind Palladian exterior; a look at the life of Lyme's Edwardian servants, English clock collection, Dutch garden, walled park high on Pennine moor.

Mam Tor, 2 miles W of Castleton: 1,700ft peak, surmounted by large Iron Age fort of 1200BC; excellent ridge walk with panoramic Peak District views between Edale and Hope Valley.

Marple: riverside town in woody ravine; moorland and woodland walks with good views. Ring O'Bells, Church Lane, popular canalside pub close to junction (on Macclesfield Canal).

Peak National Park: surrounds southern half of canal; roads criss-cross the area, giving easy access.

Poole's Cavern, Buxton Country Park: natural limestone cave, 1,000ft deep, with stalactites, stalagmites, etc; conducted tour.

Werneth Low Country Park, 3 miles N of Marple: views across to Liverpool and Welsh mountains beyond.

The Caldon Canal

From Trent and Mersey Canal at Etruria to Froghall, with branch from Hazlehurst Junction to Leek

17½ miles long, with 17 locks; Leek branch 2¾ miles long

Notable features staircase (or paired) locks at Etruria, Stockton Brook locks, Hazlehurst Junction with flyover, rural and remote setting, Froghall tunnel and terminal basin.

History Built as a branch of the Trent and Mersey Canal, and planned as an outlet for the limestone quarries at Cauldon Lowe, the Caldon Canal was opened to Froghall in 1779. Tramways linked the quarries to the canal at Froghall and trade was immediately successful. The canal flourished and at the end of the century the owners, the Trent and Mersey Company, built a branch canal to Leek. This was followed, in 1811, by another branch, from Froghall to Uttoxeter. Despite its slow and circuitous route and its many locks, the canal continued to thrive through the 19th century, and the limestone trade remained profitable until the early years of the 20th century. From the 1840s the Caldon, along with its parent, the Trent and Mersey, was railway owned, but it did not suffer from direct competition until many years later. The 20th century saw a pattern of slow decline, with the only remaining commercial traffic being the carriage of flint for grinding at the canalside mills for the pottery trade. By the 1960s the main line to Froghall was largely derelict, and the branch to Leek had been truncated. The Uttoxeter branch had been closed years before, in 1845. At this point it seemed likely that the whole canal would disappear, but its future was assured in the 1970s by the establishment of canals as leisure amenities. During the 1970s the main line was restored and reopened to Froghall.

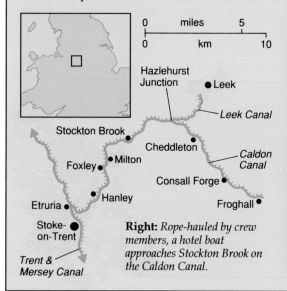

Right: *Rope-hauled by crew members, a hotel boat approaches Stockton Brook on the Caldon Canal.*

The Caldon Canal

A stretch of the Trent & Mersey links the southern end of the Macclesfield Canal, near Kidsgrove, with the Caldon Canal where it branches away, some five miles southeast, at Etruria. Just south of Kidsgrove, the Trent & Mersey enters the great black hole of the Harecastle tunnel. When opened in 1827, after three years' work, this new tunnel, designed by Thomas Telford, represented the state of the art, straight, broad and with a towpath throughout its length. Today, it is a very different story. Subsidence has caused the roof to drop in places and the towpath, having sunk beneath the water level, has been removed. Traffic is strictly one-way, the direction of flow changing at different times of day. Loading gauges at each end show boats the minimum height of the now irregular ceiling. The passage through Harecastle, as with any long canal tunnel, is slow, dark and damp, and definitely not for those who suffer from claustrophobia. The average journey will certainly take longer than crossing through the Channel Tunnel, but it is infinitely more exciting. A canal tunnel is something not to be missed.

Once away from Harecastle Hill, the main line of the Trent & Mersey Canal continues southwards

through the strange landscape of the Staffordshire Potteries. Thirty years ago, when I first saw the Trent & Mersey Canal, this was a very different landscape, a hellish vision of coal mines, a huge steel works and a skyline of smoking bottle ovens. A pall of dirt and smoke lay over the region, penetrated in places by soaring church spires. Today, all this has gone, and the few bottle ovens that remain are carefully preserved as part of a valuable heritage. The coal mines have closed and the steel works is much reduced. It is now a story of reclamation and urban regeneration, and the past has become a distant memory overlaid by auras of fantasy and romanticism. As a result, the canal journey through the Potteries is quite pleasant, and rather dull, with only occasional reminders, in the shape of old warehouses and the odd bottle oven, of the region's distinctive industrial past. The canal stays in the valley and up on the crest to the east are the great names of Arnold Bennett's Five Towns, Tunstall, Burslem and Hanley. Right by the canal is

Etruria, whose curious name is now little more than a place on a map. Until the 1950s this was the heart of the Wedgwood empire, and the factory built by the great Josiah in the 1760s stood right by the canal until it was ripped down in the 1960s. A major sponsor of the Trent & Mersey, Josiah made sure its route ran right past his factory. All that remains today is Etruria Hall, up on a hill overlooking the factory site and surrounded by the indifferent architecture spawned by one of Michael Heseltine's Garden Festivals. Two hundred years ago Josiah could sit at his breakfast table keeping an eye on his factory in the valley below.

Etruria is where the Caldon Canal branches away from the Trent & Mersey, taking a sharp turn to the left just above the Stoke flight of locks. The Caldon is a fine canal, and an unexpected haven in such gloomy surroundings. It was opened in 1779 for the same reason as the Peak Forest, namely to transport limestone, in this case from the Cauldon Lowe quarries. As with the Peak Forest, it did not actually

Above: *The Caldon Canal leaves the Trent & Mersey at Etruria, and then passes through Hanley and the distinctive architecture of the Potteries.*

reach the quarries, relying on tramways to bring the stone to the head of navigation at Froghall. Later, branches were added to Leek and Uttoxeter, establishing a busy and self-contained network that continued to thrive through the 19th century. From Etruria the Caldon rises through a series of locks to pass round the back of Hanley, a landscape of terraced houses, chimneys and corner shops relieved by the meticulous lawns, flower beds and bowling greens of Hanley Park. Suddenly, and unexpectedly, the canal reaches open countryside and the Potteries is soon a distant memory. From here onwards the Caldon is a rural delight, small scale and intimate and playing its part in an increasingly green and rolling landscape. Five attractive locks at Stockton Brook raise the canal to its summit level, 484ft above sea level and then, skirting Endon on the side of a hill, the Caldon comes to another of those wonderfully secret

stretches of waterway, inaccessible except by boat or on foot. At its heart is Denford and here the Leek branch turns away to the south, and then swings north to cross the main line on an aqueduct, a rural echo of the Macclesfield's departure from the Trent & Mersey. For a time the two canals run parallel, but at different levels, and in between a river winds its way among the trees. There is even a disused railway to add to the interest, the former mineral line to the Cauldon quarries that was the direct cause of the canal's decline. Lorries have now killed the railway, but the canal lives on in its new guise as a leisure amenity.

The Leek branch finally leaves its parent canal, to swing north along the Churnet Valley for a few miles before coming to a rather abrupt end by the aqueduct over the river. Originally it continued to a proper basin near the town, but this disappeared years ago beneath an industrial estate. However,

Opposite: *A brightly painted boat enters the top lock of the Stockton flight on the Caldon Canal. Crossing the lock is a typical iron bridge, split to allow the passage of the rope pulled by a horse.*

Left: *At Hazlehurst Junction the Caldon Canal divides, one arm going to Leek, the other to Froghall. Here, a narrow boat climbs the locks that raise the Froghall branch to the level of the Leek branch.*

Right: Polishing the brass at Froghall wharf.

Opposite: Froghall wharf, the terminus of the Caldon Canal.

there is a pleasant walk into Leek, the 'capital of the moors'. Traditionally a textile town, Leek is notable for its fine 19th-century buildings and its Arts and Crafts church, one of the best in Britain.

The main line of the Caldon follows the Churnet Valley southwards, passing the old flint mill at Cheddleton. Nearby is the revived North Staffordshire Railway, based on the splendid Jacobean-style Cheddleton Station, with the usual paraphernalia of locomotives, rolling stock and railwayana in various states of repair. The ultimate aim is the reopening of the scenic Churnet Valley railway line southwards, a not unrealistic dream considering that, a few years ago, the canal itself was abandoned and derelict. Today, the journey along the valley, with its steeply wooded walls, is a great pleasure, with river and canal side by side and actually merging for a time. Around are the traces of industry, relics that do little to spoil the canal's delightful seclusion. Consall Forge, once a busy industrial centre, is now a quiet backwater. From here the canal creeps along the wooded hillside to Froghall where a low and narrow tunnel effectively brings it to an end. It is essential, though, to walk up and over the tunnel to the real terminus beyond, a secret place hidden in the woods, with an old warehouse, huge limekilns, an old boat or two and a shop selling ice creams. It is a good place for a picnic, enjoying the smell of the wild garlic and imagining a time when the wharves were busy with boats and the kilns were hard at work turning the stone into lime. It was from here that the branch to Uttoxeter set off; the remains of the first lock can still be seen. This was a short-lived canal, one of the first casualties of the railway age. It opened in 1811, and by 1845 it was dead, with a railway built over the filled-in canal. The railway lasted longer, but has now gone the same way.

PLACES TO VISIT

Alton Towers: shell of 19th-century, battlemented mansion (some rooms restored) with landscaped gardens, engulfed in roller-coaster theme park.
Cheadle: St Giles Roman Catholic Church, 1846, a Pugin red stone masterpiece with wonderful painted interior.
Cheddleton: Flint Mill, built to grind flint for pottery industry; museum exhibits include restored horse-drawn narrow boat.
North Staffordshire Railway Centre, locomotives, railwayana, occasional rides.
Consall Forge: Nature Park, just west of canal.
Black Lion Inn, basic, popular pub in splendid canalside setting; access easier by boat than car.
Deep Hayes Country Park, near Denford: pleasant walks close to canal.
Denford: Holly Bush Inn, small traditional pub on Caldon main line, near cross-over, with access from Leek branch.
Leek: Brindley Mill and Museum, covers life of canal engineer James Brindley in his own, fully working corn mill.
All Saints' Church, superb Arts & Crafts movement church designed by Norman Shaw 1885–7.
Staffordshire Way: long-distance footpath passing through Leek, joins Caldon Canal near Horse Bridge (west of Cheddleton), leaves it at Cherry Eye Bridge, near Froghall Wharf, and continues south through Churnet Valley. See also under Macclesfield Canal Places to Visit, page 115.
Stoke-on-Trent: Chatterley Whitfield Mining Museum, underground tours, British Coal's national collection of mining artefacts. City Museum and Art Gallery, excellent collection of ceramics, social and natural history, fine art. Gladstone Pottery Museum, small Victorian pottery complete with four huge bottle ovens; demonstrations. Ceramic factory museums include Spode, Coalport, Wedgwood, Minton, Doulton.

The Leeds and Liverpool Canal

CROSSING ENGLAND horizontally is always interesting, mainly because the primary transport arteries tend to run vertically, as befits a tall, narrow country. It is harder to travel sideways, yet it is just these cross-country journeys that more sharply bring into focus the changing patterns of landscape and history. The train journey from Norwich to Liverpool is one of the best ways to see the heart of England. More revealing still are journeys that cross the country's spine. Even the insulated mindlessness of motorway travel cannot hide the impact of the Pennines. Sweeping across this barrier may seem easy, but think of the effort involved in building this broad band of tarmac. Men and great machines took years to create this trans-Pennine route. And if those men, with all their advanced technology, found it hard, think of their ancestors who, with little more than picks and shovels, built the railways across the Pennines. There are still about five lines in use, others are long closed, but the drama of their building lives on in history, legend and folk memory. As the train speeds through the rugged countryside, in and out of tunnels and cuttings, it is hard not to think about those men, the gangs of navvies, who spent years of their lives forcing railways through the inhospitable emptiness of the high Pennines.

The term navvy, short of course for navigator, is a direct link to an even earlier generation of master builders, those inland navigators who dug the canals of Britain during the last half of the 18th century. When compared with their achievements, everything pales into insignificance. Even the idea of building a waterway to carry barges across the

Two Leeds-bound narrow boats approach Greenberfield locks.

The Leeds and Liverpool Canal

From Liverpool city centre to Leeds city centre 127 miles long, with 91 broad locks

Two main branches: to Leigh and the Bridgewater Canal, 7¼ miles long, with 2 broad locks; to Tarleton and the estuary of the Douglas, 7¼ miles long, with 8 broad locks

Notable features Leeds basin and locks, Aire Valley past Kirkstall, Airedale generally, Shipley, Saltaire, Bingley and the Five-Rise staircase locks, Skipton wharves and warehouses, Greenberfield locks, Foulridge tunnel, Barrowford locks, Barnley from the embankment, Johnson's Hillock locks and junction with Walton Summit branch, Wigan lock flight and surroundings, the Rufford branch to Tarleton and the River Ribble, Liverpool docks.

History Authorised in 1770, the Leeds and Liverpool grew out of a need to expand the existing Douglas Navigation, which connected Wigan with the Ribble Estuary. John Longbotham was appointed engineer, and the first section, the lock-free stretch from Bingley to Skipton, was in use by 1773. Next came the sections from Wigan to Liverpool and from the Aire and Calder in Leeds to Gargrave, completed in 1777. These separate sections of the canal were commercially successful, but the promoters' real desire was for a trans-Pennine canal to link them together. Other trans-Pennine routes were being planned or built by this time, and so in 1790 a new Act of Parliament and new capital enabled work to be started. The Leeds and Liverpool Company was always short of money but it pressed on, and stage by stage the canal was completed, finally opening as a through route in 1816. Wisely, the directors had decided to face the extra costs imposed by broad locks, and this kept the canal profitable through the 19th century. Larger boats kept railway competition at bay, and by the end of the century the Leeds and Liverpool was the only trans-Pennine route that was still commercially viable. Its rivals closed one by one, and commercial traffic continued on parts of the canal until the 1970s. Although built as a through route, the Leeds and Liverpool was kept alive predominantly by local traffic, and by its connections, at each end, to other major commercial waterways. Today, it is a favourite long-distance cruising route, thanks to its splendidly robust engineering and the magnificence of its scenery.

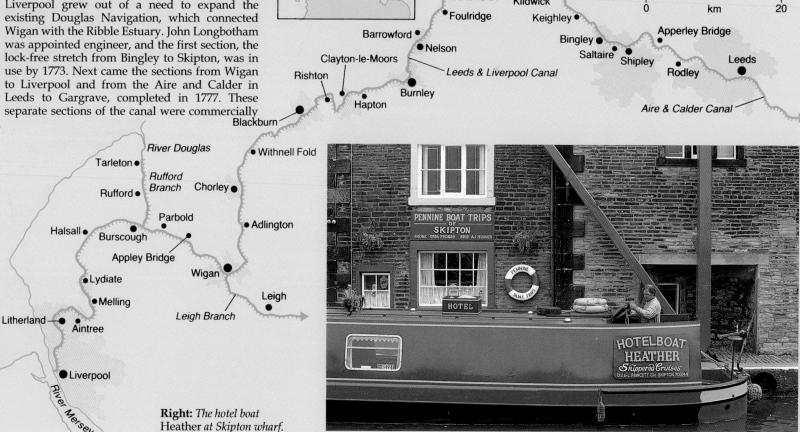

Right: *The hotel boat Heather at Skipton wharf.*

Pennines seems the height of canal mania, yet these men built not one, but three. Today, only one of these, the Leeds & Liverpool Canal, is still open to traffic, a magnificent memorial to the endeavours of the canal age.

With its end to end length of 127 miles, the Leeds & Liverpool is the longest canal in Britain, built by one company. It was also one of the most expensive, and the slowest to make, taking 40 years and costing over £1.2 million. These facts may put it in the record books, but the most surprising thing of all is that it was actually completed. The canal was not finally opened throughout until 1816, by which time its two trans-Pennine rivals, the Rochdale and the Huddersfield Narrow, had been operational for some years. This late date also put it dangerously near the railway age, yet the Leeds & Liverpool not only created its own market, but also continued to operate profitably through the 19th century despite threats posed by the various trans-Pennine railways. The main reason for this was its size. From the start it was planned as a broad canal, with locks designed to handle barges up to 60ft long and 14ft wide, and through all the vicissitudes of its construction the company rightly refused to compromise and use the standard narrow locks. The canal remained in commercial use long after the Rochdale and the Huddersfield Narrow, and it has never faced a serious closure threat. Nevertheless, the size of lock chosen was unusual and somewhat eccentric, and did not relate to much else on the British canal network. The effect of this was the development of a type of barge distinctive to the Leeds & Liverpool, the so-called Short Boat, a stocky timber-built craft that served the canal throughout its commercial life.

It may well be that the lock size was chosen by the canal's first engineer, John Longbotham, but he in turn was probably influenced by the existing river navigations in the area. The most important of these was the Douglas, made navigable in the 1730s from Wigan to the Ribble Estuary to provide an outlet to the sea for the Lancashire coalfields. This

river paved the way for, and was ultimately absorbed by, the Leeds & Liverpool. Linking as it does Lancashire and Yorkshire, the canal reflected much of the traditional rivalry between these two counties. Before a sod had been dug, there were endless arguments about the possible routes between the different groups of promoters in the two counties, and there was no final agreement until 1770, when the canal received its parliamentary authorisation. The complications of the route, its difficult and expensive engineering, the irregular supply of money, and the need to generate income quickly resulted in the canal being built in self-contained sections.

Bingley to Skipton came first, speedily built as it had no locks, then the two end sections from Leeds to Gargrave, and from Wigan to Liverpool, all open by 1777. At Wigan the line was extended by the purchase of the Douglas Navigation, as much as a source of water supply as for the trade it offered.

Above: *The distant view of Wigan, at the bottom of the flight of locks that takes the canal down through the town.*

Opposite: *A well-filled lock on the Johnson's Hill flight, with the overflow weir for excess water on the left.*

Below: *Old stone mills in Burnley, typical architecture of the Leeds & Liverpool.*

Everything then came to a halt while the company raised what income it could from its fragmented canal, and nothing much more happened until the 1790s. With a new engineer, Robert Whitworth, in charge, the company finally attacked the missing centre section. As the teams of navvies fought their way across the Pennines, yard by hard-won yard, the money drained away. Construction was constantly interrupted and so it was not until 1816 that the Leeds & Liverpool was able to fulfil the promise of its name. Despite this desperately slow start, the canal was soon operating successfully, and a number of branches increased its commercial viability. These included the Rufford branch, built to replace the now redundant Douglas Navigation, the vital Leigh branch that linked the Leeds & Liverpool to the Bridgewater Canal, and thus to Manchester, and another short link to Bradford. Coal, cloth, wool, and a variety of other cargoes ensured prosperity and the canal, thanks to its generous size, kept the railways at bay for much of the 19th century. A far greater threat was posed by problems of water supply, and these were so severe that complete closure of the canal during dry summers was not unknown. Although the engineers had tapped into every available water source on their trans-Pennine route and built reservoirs, supplies were maintained only by expensive pumping. The route was heavily locked, with 91 between Leeds and Liverpool, and these broad locks consumed water at alarming rates.

Today the Leeds & Liverpool is still a tough canal and the physical demands of its route and its large locks tend to put off those conventional boaters who see canaling as a gentle meander through pretty countryside, fuelled by regular stops at canalside pubs. Luckily, such people do not know what they are missing and so the Leeds & Liverpool is rarely crowded. It is a canal of extremes, its route linking some of the best scenery in England with dismal examples of urban and industrial decay. Its engineering is magnificent, rising easily to the challenge posed by the landscape, and it expresses better than any other waterway in Britain the 19th-century spirit of endeavour and industrial enterprise.

A journey along the Leeds & Liverpool requires a degree of commitment, in both time and attitude. It takes at least a week of long days to travel from end to end, and there is really no turning back once you have started, and no branches or junctions to offer any diversions from the route. It is a good canal for those wanting to test the strength of their relationships with their loved ones, their family or their friends; it has a reputation for either breaking them or sealing them for good. At first sight, a few days on a canal boat, drifting through a landscape dappled with soft sunlight, sounds idyllic, rating pretty high on the romance stakes, and I am sure many couples have set off together into what they assumed would be a sunset of blissful togetherness. And that is often the problem, for the togetherness is unremitting. A canal boat offers no privacy, and

Above: *Boatmen at Greenberfield locks.*

this everything you possess is sodden and streaked with mud, and somehow it always seems to spread everywhere.

Secondly, there is the tiredness. Travelling along a canal is physically demanding, and your body is soon aching from the effort of doing all sorts of things that involve muscles you did not know you had. For the first few days complete exhaustion and all-pervading dampness can put a complete end to any ideas of romance. After that you begin to feel wonderfully fit, but by then the danger period will have passed and either you will have worked out a *modus vivendi* with your companion or she (or he) will have abandoned ship and gone home. Most canals are quite near railway lines and I am sure the end of many a beautiful friendship has been marked by a long solitary wait on a remote station.

Thirdly, there is the problem of hygiene. Boats do have washing facilities, and some even claim to have showers, although the appeal of contorting yourself into a tiny cupboard under a lukewarm drip is somewhat limited. The thing about water on a boat is that you have to remember to put it into the tank in the first place, and the 50 or so gallons that most boats seem to carry disappears very quickly if you behave as you would at home. Filling the tank involves wrestling with a long, wet hose, and plenty of standing about in the rain, and you soon learn to do it as rarely as possible. The net result of all this is that regular washing quickly goes out of the window. After a few days dirt is universal and hands are ingrained with mud and grease, and covered with blisters from winding the lock windlass and pulling on ropes. Gentle fondling in a suggestive manner with hands in this condition is rarely welcomed. Further difficulties of an intimate nature are caused by canal boat lavatories, or rather the lack of them. Some boats do have apparently ordinary flushing lavatories which discharge themselves into some ghastly tank in the bowels of the vessel. Anyone who has ever had to empty such a tank would certainly never use one again, and the same applies to the so-called

the only way to get away is to jump off, and go for a long walk. Everything is shared, 24 hours a day, and everything is public. It is best therefore to travel with old friends whose awful habits are well known and easily tolerated. The temptation to take a new lover for a romantic interlude on the canal should always be resisted, for the strains imposed by the intimacies of canal boat life can be terminal. Romance and the journey are generally quite incompatible.

First, there is the weather. Despite all one's hopes and expectations, it will generally rain. Rain brings mud, and wet clothes, and few boats have adequate drying spaces. Someone has to steer all the time, and a canal boat steerer stands at the stern, fully exposed to everything the weather can chuck down. Someone else has to work the locks, make cups of tea, go shopping, cook the dinner, and carry out a range of other activities that involve continuous movement on and off the boat. After a few days of chemical toilet, another horrific contrivance which has to be emptied far more often, and refilled with a pernicious blue liquid that kills everything it touches. The tried and tested method, favoured by serious boatmen since time immemorial, is a bucket and a spade, the former to be used at night or during periods of bad weather, and the latter as a necessary accompaniment for solitary walks into the secluded corners of the nearby countryside. Traditionally known as bucket and chuck it, this old technique is rarely used nowadays, but even this simple system can cause unexpected difficulties. One cold and deeply foggy night, I went ashore and dug a large hole in what I took to be a remote field, miles from anywhere. I returned to the boat, moored nearby, and went to bed. The next morning was bright and clear, and I was horrified to see that what I had taken to be a field was actually somebody's front lawn, and the signs of my visit were all too clear. There was nothing for it but to untie the ropes and sail away, with what can only be called indecent haste. For some, all these methods are equally unacceptable, and they have to wait, with increasing discomfort, for the next pub. There are, of course, boats lavishly equipped with baths and proper showers, impressive water heating devices, and suitably huge water tanks, but the price of such luxury is the need to devote what seems like hours each day to filling these tanks. Unless there is a paid crew – and few canal boats run to that – most people slip quickly and quietly into the state of general dirtiness, happy in the knowledge that everyone else is in the same boat.

Being a long and, in many places, isolated canal, the Leeds & Liverpool will bring such matters to the fore, but they should not be allowed to put anyone off what is a most exciting journey. Everyone who likes canals must, at some point, do the Leeds & Liverpool, but it should not be the first choice for someone seeking the perfect setting for a romantic interlude. The only answer to this problem is to moor the boat in some quiet spot, preferably not too far away from necessary facilities, and stay there for

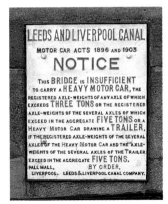

Above: *Cast iron canal company notice in Leeds.*

Below: *Boats moored by the railway bridge near Office lock in Leeds. In the foreground is a converted short boat, the characteristic barge of the Leeds & Liverpool.*

some days. In such circumstances, it does not really matter which canal it is, and the boat might as well not even leave the marina.

The start of the Leeds & Liverpool is in the recently restored city centre, where River lock marks the meeting point of this canal and the Aire & Calder. Leeds is one of those places that looks good from the water, and the canal's route westwards out of the city is interesting and attractive against the background of powerful 19th-century mills and warehouses. The locks start immediately, and there is no respite from here to the summit high in the Pennines. From Leeds the canal follows the Aire Valley, sticking firmly to the wooded southern side as the valley narrows. The dark stone walls of ruined Kirkstall Abbey add an element of the picturesque, and an echo of the former importance of the Aire as a transport artery in the Middle Ages. The canal follows tenaciously the river's winding course through a dramatic landscape of wooded hills, dark stone buildings,

Opposite: The flight of five locks at Bingley with Saltaire in the distance.

Below: *The Italianate mills of Saltaire, the 'ideal' industrial town built by Sir Titus Salt.*

and fine views, scenery typical of the route as a whole. Its physical character is quickly apparent, with plenty of locks, often in groups of two or three, interspersed with heavy swing bridges. The surroundings are equally strong, and from Shipley westwards great stone mills with their towering chimneys dominate the countryside. Climbing continuously, the canal makes its way through this dark satanic landscape that brings to life the vitality of the textile trade in the Victorian period. It was the trade generated by these mills that kept the canal busy at a time when its rivals were in decline. At Shipley is the junction with the former Bradford Canal, little of which remains. Opened in 1774, closed in the 1860s, opened again in 1873, and closed for ever in 1922, this short waterway was notorious for its pollution. Apparently the water was so tainted with chemicals and muck in the mid-Victorian period that it gave off noxious gases that would burn with a blue flame. Sometimes the whole surface of the canal would be quietly aflame.

The most exciting place, set right on the canal, is Saltaire, Sir Titus Salt's ideal industrial village. It looks much the same as when it was built in the 1850s, and Victorian philanthropy still pervades the atmosphere. At the centre is the great mill, now used for various commercial and cultural activities, and all around is Salt's new town with workers' houses, shops, institute, school, but, in his day, no pubs, all in the same strong Renaissance-inspired architectural style. He also built the grand Italianate church, creating a total community that reflected a pioneering awareness of the links between quality of life and quantity of output.

After Saltaire, the canal crosses the Aire on the seven-arched Dowley Gap aqueduct, and then comes Bingley, a mill town with a difference. Here, grouped tightly together, are eight locks, and five of them are together in a daunting, near vertical staircase. Staircase locks, where the top gate of one lock forms the bottom gate of the next and so on, were commonly built in the late 18th century to save construction costs in hilly terrain, but most are only two or three locks. Only at Bingley is there the justly famous Five-Rise staircase. Many a boatman has gone pale when faced by this daunting piece of engineering, and you need to be both fit and sharp-witted to pass through it successfully. Operating the paddles in the wrong order can leave the boat stranded or cause spectacular floods. I remember seeing a fisherman, innocently going about his business, seated by the canal with his mind miles away, being suddenly swept almost into the bushes by a tidal wave released by an incompetent lock operator far above.

Bingley's top lock marks the start of a long and notably attractive 16-mile lock-free stretch. This is Airedale at its best, fine moorland views framed by steep green hills, and broken by dark stone towns and villages. On a distant crest is Keighley, one mile south from the canal, but worth the walk whose start is marked by East Riddlesden Hall, a 17th-century manor right by the canal. Not to be missed, as much for the landscape as anything else,

Above: *Gardens and mills accompany the canal through Silsden.*

loaded, via long chutes, straight onto the boats waiting below. Near Gargrave the locks start again, lifting the canal out of Airedale, even though it still follows closely the river's meanderings. All around is the moorland landscape of the Yorkshire Dales National Park, and long views to the distant 1,000ft fells form a spectacular backdrop. Another aqueduct crosses over the Aire again, and then the locks come thick and fast, as the canal twists and turns alarmingly on its climb to its summit. At East Marton the Pennine Way passes briefly along the towpath on its 150-mile route from Edale northwards. This well-trodden long-distance path is almost too well-known nowadays, and a good way to see the Pennines without the crowds is to walk the Leeds & Liverpool towpath, particularly in this area. Greenberfield top lock marks the start of the summit. As so often, the engineers made a serious error here, for the six-mile summit is far too short to ensure good supplies of water for the locks, despite the reservoirs, and in conditions of dry summer weather this section is notorious for water shortages. From the earliest days, summer closures were not uncommon, a factor that encouraged the development of local traffic rather than regular long-distance use.

After skirting Barnoldswick, the canal comes to its one major tunnel. A canal tunnel is always a treat and, while at 1,640yds Foulridge is by no means the longest in England, it is still exciting. Narrow, and with no towpath, this rocky bore presents a sinister spectacle, and the passage through it is filled with the ghosts of those gangs of navvies who carved it out of the hill, and of those generations of boatmen who, painfully, slowly and hour by hour legged their barges through the darkness by walking along the walls. Until the arrival of the steam tugs in 1880, this was the only way through. Foulridge is also famous for the cow incident of 1912, when a particularly stupid animal fell into the canal at the tunnel's western end and then proceeded to swim all the way through to the other end, where it was revived by swigs of brandy.

is the Keighley & Worth Valley Steam Railway, a line made famous by the film *The Railway Children*. The Airedale villages make the most of the canal. Silsden has fine old warehouses, while Kildwick, with its steep streets of stone cottages, has the canal, a swing bridge and an aqueduct right at its heart. The views along the valley from this part of the canal are simply magnificent, and justify all that exercise at the locks.

Skipton, with its Norman castle and 14th-century church, encompasses centuries of British history, but it is also central to the history of the Leeds & Liverpool. It was here in the Black Horse Hotel that the canal company held its inaugural meeting, and the town was at the heart of the first section to be completed. Around the wharf are fine 1770s warehouses, and the whole town still carries the aura of that time. Lovers of the picturesque should not miss the short Springs branch, a short arm that runs below the castle walls and into a steep rock cutting that is virtually a ravine, built in the 18th century to allow stone from the local quarry to be

Left: A modern hire boat negotiates the Bank Newton locks.

Foulridge represents the watershed, and soon after the tunnel the Barrowford locks mark the start of the long descent. The surroundings become more industrial as the canal passes Nelson, but the distant views are dominated by the high bulk of Pendle Hill, across the Calder Valley. This satisfies not only the visual senses, but also the imagination, being long associated with witches. Sharp bends then take the canal round Burnley, with memorable views of the town spread over the hillside below. At this point the canal is carried 60ft above the town on a huge embankment, pierced at the centre by an aqueduct. Another tunnel, Gannow, takes it below the Burnley suburbs and out into the more open landscape of the Calder Valley. Lacking the spectacular quality of the Yorkshire scenery, this stretch has none the less a bleakness that is

Photographs in the local pub, The Hole in the Wall, confirm the truth of this apparently apochryphal story. In fact, cows and canals do not get on that well together, despite their constant proximity. Cows clearly do not understand boats at all, and often come to grief when trying to get a drink from the canal, either getting stuck in the mud or being unable to get out again because they cannot remember where they went in. On one occasion my crew had the greatest difficulty in rescuing a calf that had fallen, or wandered, into the canal, and then found itself unable to climb back out because of the concrete piling that, unusually, flanked both banks. Even calves are very heavy, and the combined efforts of the four of us could not lift it out, not that it was doing much to help itself. In the end the farmer had to be summoned and he, less concerned than us about the animal's comfort, roughly hauled it out and then drove it back towards its field with a kick.

Right: *Narrow boats and sheep at Greenberfield locks.*

attractive, particularly against the distant views of moorland. It is a tough and uncompromising landscape, open country contrasting with millstone grit and the legacy of centuries of industrial exploitation. Raw cotton and machinery were the stable cargoes of the canal, from here down to Liverpool docks, and they have left their mark. Blackburn looks best from a distance, when at least 12 church spires can be counted, not to mention all the towering chimneys. Locks drop the canal through the city centre, and then it leaves on a raised embankment, offering good views for sports enthusiasts, who can choose between white-suited lady bowls players or the more colourful garb, and play, of the Rovers.

Past the industrial estate village of Withnell Fold, built to serve local mills once famous for the making of banknote paper, the canal reaches Wheelton and the Johnson's Hill flight of locks. At the bottom is the junction with all that remains of the Walton Summit branch. In the early days of the Leeds & Liverpool, the company saved money by sharing its route from here to Wigan with the Lancaster Canal, who had previously built this section as part of their main line towards Preston, and from there onwards to Lancaster and Kendal. Their original plan was also to extend southwards to join the Bridgewater Canal but, desperately short of money, they never completed the project, and the Leeds & Liverpool had to pick up the pieces. They did not do much better going north, for the canal stopped three miles from Johnson's Hill, and never made it to Preston as they could not afford the cost of the aqueduct across the Ribble. Instead, they built, in 1803, a five-mile tramway to connect their two canals either side of Preston, which crossed the Ribble on a trestle bridge. This 'temporary' expedient was never replaced and lasted until its

Left: *Old stone mills flanking the canal at Burnley.*

Right: *Waiting for the lock to fill on the Johnson's Hill flight.*

final closure in the 1870s, involving gangs of labourers in complicated transhipment operations between the tramway and the two parts of the canal.

Woods and farmland, and generally pleasant country accompany the canal past Chorley, with the M61 making its presence felt only briefly. It is a predominantly rural landscape, but there are plenty of echoes of industry, notably the overgrown remains of former coalmines, while mansions such as Haigh Hall and Arley Hall reflect the wealth generated by this long industrial past. Ahead is Wigan and the long flight of 21 locks that drops the canal over 200ft in a couple of miles. The view from the top used to look out over a mass of smoking chimneys and dark factories, scattered with the spoil tips and winding gear of the mines, but now it is very different, and the Orwellian vision of Wigan has been put firmly into the history books. Even Wigan Pier is now a tourist attraction rather than a music hall joke; it did actually exist, as the landing stage for fly boats that, in the pre-railway age, operated regular passenger services to Liverpool. The lock flight is lined with pubs and old working men's clubs, and it was from these that there issued gangs of old men called 'hufflers' who, for the price of a drink, would help with the arduous labour of the locks.

Right: *Trip boat maintenance at Wigan Pier.*

Most people end their Leeds & Liverpool cruise at Wigan, for from there to Liverpool the canal's route is marked by a steady and progressive decline from the pleasant to the downright dangerous. The main line from Wigan turns northwest and then south to run parallel to the coast. At one point it is only four miles from the sea at Southport. South from Wigan is the branch to Leigh, where it meets the Bridgewater Canal, completing the section of the route planned by the Lancaster Canal Company. Another branch runs northwards from Burscough, along the line of the old Douglas Navigation, to Tarleton. Known as the Rufford Branch, this joins the Ribble Estuary via the tidal section of the Douglas. A once busy waterway, it is now a delightful exploration of a forgotten landscape of low-lying fields framed by tall reeds. It is always exciting when a canal finally meets the sea, and the contrast between the two styles of boating becomes apparent. On its way north the canal passes Rufford Old Hall, a 15th-century timber-framed mansion, and its 18th-century replacement, the New Hall. This is a remote and little used waterway, and a lucky boat may be rewarded by the sight of the Old Grey Lady leaving the Old Hall and drifting across the canal on a bridge that no longer exists.

The main line down to Liverpool offers excitements and drama of a different kind. The route into the city is via Scarisbrick, notable for its A W Pugin mansion, Lydiate, Aintree, where racegoers will be familiar with the Canal Turn, and Litherland. The progression is from open countryside to suburbia and from this to industry and urban squalor. Those who promoted the canal in the 1770s were not to know what would happen two centuries later, or that their chosen route would end up as one of the most notorious in Britain. A canal guide written in the early 1970s describes the primary hazard as 'urchins throwing stones'. Today, a boat would be lucky indeed to escape so lightly. It is a pity, and a great waste, for what could be better than to sail into Liverpool's regenerated docks at the helm of one's own canal boat, dropping down the four locks of the Stanley Dock branch, and completing the journey planned so long ago by a group of local businessmen meeting in that pub in Skipton.

Above: *Decorative cast iron details at Wigan Pier.*

PLACES TO VISIT

Bradford: see under Aire & Calder Canal Places to Visit, page 43.

Chorley: Astley Hall, a timber-framed 16th-century house in 99 acres of park and woodland.

Gawthorpe Hall, 3 miles NW of Burnley, near Padiham: built in 1600 and restored by Charles Barry in the 1850s; portraits from the National Portrait Gallery and Kay Shuttleworth textile collections (National Trust).

Haskayne: Ship, well-known and attractive canalside pub.

Keighley: Cliffe Castle Museum, French furniture from the V & A, local and natural history.

East Riddlesden Hall, set close to the canal, a traditional 17th-century West Yorkshire manor house with Yorkshire oak furniture, pewter etc; walled garden restored to original design, large medieval tithe barn (National Trust).

Keighley & Worth Valley Railway, runs 4¾ miles from Keighley (also BR) through Brontë country to Haworth (for Brontë Parsonage Museum) and on to Oxenhope.

Leeds: see under Aire & Calder Canal, page 43.

Liverpool: sights include Tate Gallery Liverpool, home of the National Collection of Modern Art in the north, the Walker Art Gallery's excellent collection of European painting and sculpture, the Merseyside Maritime Museum in the revived docklands, Animation World's exhibition of cartoon and animation, and The Beatles Story.

Martin Mere, 2 miles NW of Burscough Bridge: Wildfowl & Werlands Trust reserve outstanding for its visiting waders and wildfowl.

Rufford Old Hall: timber-framed Tudor hall notable for its ornate hammerbeam roof; tapestries, 16th-century arms and armour, and 17th-century oak furniture (National Trust).

Saltaire: Salt's Mill, the 1853 Gallery displays over 300 works by Bradford-born David Hockney.

Scarisbrick: Heatons Bridge, a basic and genuinely traditional canalside pub.

Skipton: Castle, one of the most complete medieval castles in England, originally Norman, rebuilt in the 1650s; moat, dungeon, 50ft banqueting hall.

Church of Holy Trinity, in front of the castle, 14th-century and battlemented, notable for its oak roof and heavily carved font cover.

Royal Shepherd, lively pub overlooking the Springs branch of the canal.

Southport: Atkinson Art Gallery, 19th- and 20th-century paintings and prints.

Southport Railway Centre, large collection of ex-British Rail and industrial locomotives, tramcars, buses and traction engines.

Wigan Pier: wharf and warehouses revamped as a museum of life at the turn of the century, with mock-ups of a coal mine, pub, miner's house, school; waterbus or canalside walk connects to a restored textile mill.

The Llangollen Canal

T HE LLANGOLLEN CANAL, or, to use its correct title, the Llangollen branch of the Shropshire Union Canal, is one of the most extraordinary waterways in Britain. The idea of constructing a canal that reached deep into the mountainous heart of North Wales, to serve a remote region with very little industry, must have seemed on the face of it absurd. Yet, the canal mania that gripped British speculators at the end of the 18th century threw up many schemes even more impractical than this. Most of these never left the drawing board. A few went as far as to receive their Act of Authorisation from Parliament. Very few indeed were ever completed, although there are cases where short and isolated stretches of grandiose schemes were actually built. The Grand Western Canal is one, where all that was constructed of the ambitious Exeter to Bristol route was an 11-mile section near Tiverton. And this took up four years, and cost more than the total sum estimated for the whole canal. Not surprisingly, things did not go much further, although the canal did finally reach Taunton in 1838, just in time for a very few years' use before the railways took all the traffic. An even better example is the grandly named Kington, Leominster & Stourport Canal, a scheme to link the remoter parts of rural Herefordshire to the River Severn, and thus to the industrial heartlands of England. The primary cargoes were to be agricultural produce, although there may have been some idea that the canal's existence might encourage the spread of industrialisation into an area that was notable, then as now, for its lack of industry. This patently ridiculous scheme went

The Cheshire Plain, with Hurleston Junction in the foreground, where the Llangollen leaves the Shropshire Union.

145

The Llangollen Canal

From Hurleston in Cheshire, on the Shropshire Union main line, to Llantisilio, near Llangollen 46 miles long, with 21 locks

The partly restored Montgomery branch runs from Frankton to Newtown, 35 miles long, with 25 locks

Notable features Hurleston Junction and locks, Wrenbury, lift bridges, Ellesmere town, basin and nearby meres, the Montgomery Canal southwards from Frankton, Chirk aqueduct, Pontcysyllte aqueduct, Dee Valley landscape, Llangollen, Llantisilio and Horseshoe Falls.

History One of the most popular canals in Britain, the Llangollen is busier now than it ever was during its complicated history as a commercial waterway. What exists today as an attractive branch of the Shropshire Union was born out of various plans by 18th-century speculators to develop the town of Chester as a port. First came the Chester Canal Company, set up in 1772 to build a canal from Chester on the Dee to the Trent & Mersey at Middlewich, and thus to link Chester, and the Mersey, to the Severn via the national network. This was completed to Nantwich by 1779, but never really got much further. Next there was the Ellesmere Company, whose plan for a canal from Chester to Shrewsbury on the Severn via Ruabon and Ellesmere was launched in 1791. Work began two years later, and by 1806 the company had completed 48 miles of canal and developed Ellesmere Port on the Mersey. However, the Chester to Shrewsbury main line, with its Dee and Severn connections, was never completed, and the Ellesmere was a completely self-contained network on the Welsh borders, its only connection to the outside world being its junction at Hurleston with the Chester Canal. Within this enclosed system lay the Llangollen Canal, partly a section of the proposed main line, and partly branches, eastwards to Hurleston, and westwards to Llangollen and Llantisilio, the latter being essentially a navigable feeder to ensure good supplies of water. The Chester and Ellesmere companies finally merged in 1813, but they never completed their proposed routes southwards. Eventually the Trent & Mersey connection was made at Middlewich, but too late to fulfil the original promoters' expectations. The main route south was not completed until 1835, and then by another company altogether, the Birmingham & Liverpool Junction. In 1845 this whole complex network was merged into the Shropshire Union Railways and Canal Company, who operated it successfully through the 19th century, despite increasing railway competition. Serious and rapid decline followed the First World War, and one by one branches were abandoned. An Act of 1944 formally closed 178 miles of the Shropshire Union network, but the Llangollen survived because of its importance as a source of water supply. With the development of leisure boating, the Llangollen's obvious appeal quickly took it to the top of the league.

Above: *Typical lift bridge, on the Prees branch.*

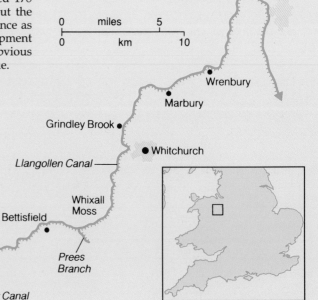

Above: *Canal signpost at Frankton Junction.*

ahead none the less, the Act was passed, money was raised and the engineer Thomas Dadford produced plans for an obviously expensive and ambitious route which included four long tunnels, three large aqueducts, and over 60 locks. The estimated cost for this folly was £150,000, a sum apparently raised locally without undue difficulties. After protracted difficulties, an isolated 18-mile length of canal was finally opened from Leominster to Southnet. This absorbed most of the capital, and little more was ever done. The canal was closed by 1859. Needless to say, no dividend was ever paid, and the shareholders all lost their money. Much of it must have been used to create the canal's most eccentric feature, a tunnel that never saw the passage of a boat. This, 1,250yds long, was built at great expense east of Southnet, the first part of the planned route towards Stourport. It was completed in 1795, promptly collapsed, and was never touched again. There it still lies, entombed and unseen, the classic case of a poor investment.

It is all the more remarkable, therefore, that the Llangollen Canal was not only planned, but actually completed as planned. It would be an understatement to call its history labyrinthine. Now one of the most popular cruising waterways in Britain, the Llangollen owes its origins to a number of separate late 18th-century canal schemes. The first of these was the Chester Canal, whose proposed route from Chester to Middlewich on the Trent & Mersey was authorised in 1772. The inspiration, and the money, came from local businessmen who wanted Chester to rival Liverpool as a port. The canal reached Nantwich in 1779 but progressed no further, and it took another 50 years to make the connection with the Trent & Mersey. Meanwhile, another scheme to connect the Mersey and the Severn had appeared. This was the Ellesmere Canal, and between 1796 and 1806 it was able to bring to fruition many parts of its plans, including the development of the new dock complex at Ellesmere Port, on the Mersey, part of the main line southwards, and a series of branches

reaching out into Wales. Of the main line south from Chester to Ruabon, Ellesmere and Shrewsbury, little was finished, for the company soon decided instead to build a branch from Frankton to join the Chester Canal at Hurleston. The completed parts of the main line, from Weston northwards to Frankton, and from Frankton to Pontcysyllte, therefore became branches with the latter part of the route extended to Llangollen and Llantisilio. Later, it all became part of the Shropshire Union network, which remained busy and profitable through the 19th century. The other strange thing about the Llangollen is that it was never really planned as a proper full-scale navigation. Hurleston to Pontcysyllte was always, as the planned main line, a proper canal, but the extension westwards from Pontcysyllte to Llangollen and Llantisilio was built by the Ellesmere Company as a feeder, to keep their network supplied with water by drawing on the fast-flowing and reliable higher reaches of the Dee.

Above: *Sheltering from the rain in Chirk tunnel.*

Opposite. The canal nears its terminus at Llantisilio.

For various reasons it was decided that this should be a navigable feeder, and so the waterway built to reach the Horseshoe Falls was made just large enough for boats. Herein lies the reason for its continued existence. In 1944 much of the Shropshire Union's extensive network of canals was formally adandoned, including all the canals in Wales except the Llangollen. This was kept open, for the whole canal system of the region, not to mention the Cheshire water supply, could not operate without the six million gallons a day of River Dee water that it carries southwards.

With its mountainous route, magnificent engineering and spectacular scenery, the Llangollen is understandably a favourite. At the height of the season journey times can be greatly extended and long queues at the locks are a regular feature. Progress is in any case limited by the fact that this is one of the few canals that has a perceptible current, with the result that it takes far longer to travel from Hurleston to Llangollen than the other way round. It is a canal completely incompatible with any sense of urgency, imposing its own timescale upon all who visit it. The quick dash approach, simply to cross it off the list, is wholly out of place, and completely impractical.

The temptation therefore, is to visit the canal out of season. Not only can the scenery look even better then, but noticeable by their absence are the fleets of hire cruisers, many of which are inevitably crewed by people who are on a canal for the first time and really do not have a clue. Entertaining though their antics can be, even these begin to pall with constant repetition. The canal, luckily, has a wonderful way of reasserting its natural authority. It is not unknown, unfortunately, for certain groups to travel along with portable radios blaring, an anti-social habit at the best of times, and at its worst on the quiet of a canal. I remember a particularly noisy boat making its way along the canal near Hurleston, with a transistor on the bow drowning out every other sound. As the boat swung round a bend, one of the two plump girls lounging by the radio shifted her position, rolled her ample Levi's-covered bottom into the tranny, and toppled it into the water. For a very few seconds the muffled tones of Radio One could just be heard, and then there was a delightful silence, broken briefly by the shrill shrieks of the girls who then, mercifully, went below to sulk.

Dropping things over the side is a feature of canal life, and can happen to the most experienced of boaters. I have seen cups of coffee and sometimes a complete plate of lunch inadvertently swept into the canal from a hazardous perch on the cabin roof. Hats are always sailing off, but at least these can be retrieved by a burst of well-timed reversing and skilful use of the boathook. The most common losses are the iron windlasses used to operate the locks. There must be stretches of canal completely paved with these, and their constant loss must give great cheer to windlass manufacturers. Equally common is the habit of putting the things down somewhere when the paddle winding process is finished, and then leaving them behind when getting back in the boat. Traditionally, boatmen carried them stuck into the backs of their belts, and this is still a good idea. Other bits of gear commonly lost over the side include iron mooring stakes and

Below: Winding up a paddle at Marbury lock.

the detachable chimneys used on boats equipped with stoves, often detached in an unpleasant fashion by the curve of a low bridge. Maps and guides are common victims of sudden gusts of wind. Anyone who has experienced this will be familiar with one of those basic rules of life, namely that a sodden Ordnance Survey map will never fold properly again, however carefully it is dried, and that the bit you actually need will always be the bit that is now illegible.

Many canals are at their best out of season, and the Llangollen is undoubtedly one of them. Its route high on the sides of the hills makes the most of the colours of early spring and autumn, and the clarity of light greatly improves the views. In the right circumstances the bare trees of winter can also be exciting, particularly if there is snow on the distant summits. The right circumstances mean a boat equipped with a stove, kept roaring on the plentiful supplies of wood to be found by any canal. Finding suitable wood and then cutting it up into neat lengths to be stacked by the fire is a great pleasure, with all its attendant illusions of self-sufficiency. The stove glows, the sweet-smelling smoke drifts away, and the stew bubbles on the hotplate. The smoke is not so good when you are steering and it is blowing, as it always seems to be, in your face. A day of this and you feel, and smell, like an old kipper. The warmth of the stove is a delight, especially at night, but it is a very hot iron box in a very confined space. Once a friend, admittedly rather large, while backing out of the tiny washing space which faced the stove, placed his naked buttocks against the oven door, with very painful results.

A bottle of whisky is also essential equipment for winter travelling, although excessive use can cause problems. A long time ago, a friend and I travelled many miles through the dark night of a canal in winter, sustained by ample supplies of this vital fluid. Eventually, with the bottle nearly empty, it was time to stop. We moored the boat and went to bed, only to fall into a furious argument. My friend was sure we were moored on the left bank, while I was certain we were lying on the right. Eventually, exhausted by the dispute, we decided that we had moored diagonally across the canal, and were therefore both right. Having reached this satisfactory compromise, we slept deeply. Crawling on to the deck in the bright sun of a winter s morning, I was relieved to find the boat neatly moored beside the towpath, exactly as it should have been.

Canal cooking is a particular art, demanding as it does a confident mastery of the stove. Only cowards will fall back on tins and packets, while the more adventurous will go in for breadmaking, and the creation of exotic and demanding culinary treats. For middle of the road cooks, the canal stew is a reliable standby. It can be quickly prepared between locks, and then left to its own devices in the stove. Ingredients can be constantly varied, and the same stew can, with occasional additions, be made to last indefinitely. One friend, planning to spend many weeks on the canals, but lamenting that his lack of cooking ability would force him into an unwelcome familiarity with fish and chips, meals in baskets and provincial curries, was taught the basic canal stew. He set off, much cheered, and when I visited a couple of weeks later he served a very passable stew. My next visit was not for some weeks, and it was stew again. There had clearly been developments, but I am still pretty sure that the tough and unchewable piece of gristle I found on that occasion bore an uncanny resemblance to one I had come across on my first visit, several weeks before.

The difficulties of cooking are often made worse by the smallness of the stove, and the lack of space. One winter's night I had prepared a masterpiece of a stew, and the freezing crew members on duty at the helm were being driven into ecstasies of anticipation by the smells wafting up from the cabin. It was a wet night, and the comings and goings that inevitably accompany any passage through locks had left a liberal deposit of sticky

Above: *The basin and old Shropshire Union warehouse at Ellesmere.*

Opposite: *A typical Llangollen landscape near Whitchurch.*

mud over the cabin floor. I went down to give the stew a final stir and pulled the pot out of the oven. At that point, some law of canal dynamics caused it to fall from my hands, turn over in the air, and empty its contents over the muddy floor. This was disaster on a grand scale. Deprived of their dinner, and with no fish and chip shop or pub for miles, my crew would, I knew, throw me into the canal. Taking care that I could not be seen from the deck, I scooped and scraped the stew, now liberally mixed with mud, from the floor and back into the pot. Returning it to the oven, I announced that supper would be ready in ten minutes, hoping that this would be sufficient time at least to discourage some of the germs now inextricably added to it. We duly ate the stew, and all agreed it was one of the best.

The route of the Llangollen is like a good play, with a slow start that builds up over several acts to a spectacular climax. Hurleston Junction is surrounded by the typical green and lush farmland of north Cheshire, quiet, remote and well away from the main roads. In canal terms though, this is

the main road, with several hundred boats a week using the Llangollen at the peak of the season. Immediately after leaving the main line of the Shropshire Union, boats encounter the four Hurleston locks, and it is here that the queues can start. It is usually quite orderly, with boats alternately moving up and down the locks, but there are always those who through incompetence, impatience, or sheer bloody-mindedness make life difficult. It is entertaining to watch, but frustrating if you are stuck further back in the queue. An early start is always a good idea, for many holiday boaters cannot seem to get going until the galley slaves have produced a very full cooked breakfast.

The first few miles of the Llangollen are quiet and pretty, with small and remote villages, isolated locks and lift bridges, of the type associated with Van Gogh, establishing its distinctive character. It is at its most appealing at Wrenbury, where the wharf and lift bridge are overshadowed by old warehouses and a mill. Nearby is Marbury, another fine village whose attractive church stands above a little lake. As the canal nears Whitchurch through a flight of locks, the broad valley of farmland begins to narrow, hinting at the more dramatic landscape that lies ahead. The handsome town of Whitchurch is set to the east, originally reached via a short branch canal which was filled in years ago. One of the Llangollen's main attractions is the constantly changing landscape, and on its route to Ellesmere, criss-crossing the Welsh border, farmland is replaced by old peat bogs and small lakes, or meres, the latter often set among moorland. An old and disused branch leads away towards Prees, one of a number built in the early 19th century for agricultural cargoes. Ellesmere itself, preceded by a short tunnel, is set at the end of a short arm, where the basin is still surrounded by fine canal warehouses. It is difficult today to associate this quiet market town with the great industrial centre and complex of locks at Ellesmere Port, yet when the canal was built Ellesmere was one of the major towns along the route, and the new port created

Opposite: *The grand aqueduct at Chirk, with the later railway viaduct alongside.*

from nothing near the tiny Merseyside hamlet of Netherpool was named after it.

At Frankton there is the junction with the Montgomery Canal. This was originally built by the Ellesmere Company as a branch to Llanymynech, but was gradually extended southwards by two separate companies, finally reaching Newtown in 1821. As in so many other cases, this was a canal that never fulfilled the hopes of its sponsors, or paid its way. It was one of the many rural canals whose existence was largely based upon lime. Limestone was carried to the canalside kilns and the lime that resulted was transported to and fro to serve the needs of farmers. It sounds a most precarious existence, and often was, but today it is easy to forget the importance of lime as a fertiliser.

After a serious breach near Frankton in 1936 effectively closed the canal, the Montgomery was gradually abandoned, and its attractive 35-mile route lay derelict for years. Today, an ambitious restoration project is gradually bringing it back to life, and a number of sections are now completed. However, full navigation is limited by a series of dropped main road bridges. I walked the whole canal in 1969 over a rather arduous weekend, and it was entertainingly varied. Some stretches were in good order, full of water, and gave the impression that the last boat had passed only weeks before, but elsewhere the canal had completely vanished, its route no more than a grassy depression across a field. It was a journey full of the picturesque, with derelict locks, crumbling aqueducts, overgrown bridges and, from time to time, the skeletons of narrow boats long forgotten in the bushes, filled with reeds and wild flowers. One had formerly been *The Berriew,* built in the 19th century as a passenger-carrying express fly boat. Fly boats were a feature of many canals until the railways took over, offering scheduled services with speeds guaranteed by regular changes of towing horses. They had right of way over the lumbering cargo boats; some carried a knife mounted on the bow to cut through the towing ropes of anything that got in the way. In some ways the Montgomery was more appealing as the romantic ruin it was when I walked it 25 years ago, a secret whose pleasures were revealed only to those prepared to make the effort to find the lost route. The enthusiasm that drives the canal restorer forever onwards is understandable, but this was a canal that was never going anywhere, and could well have been left in that state.

It is the next session of the Llangollen that justifies its great popularity. As it approaches the mountains, the route twists and turns, in and out of cuttings high on the side of the steep hill. Suddenly, turning a corner, the canal seems to leave the ground, carried high in the air on the golden stone arches of the Chirk aqueduct. Beside it is the taller viaduct carrying the railway, added after John Sell Cotman had painted his famous watercolour that makes the aqueduct into a towering triumphant arch, a celebration of man's conquest of nature in

Below: *Leaving the short tunnel at Ellesmere.*

Above: *A boat flies high across the Dee, carried on Telford's magnificent iron trough aqueduct at Pontcysyllte.*

the spirit of early 19th-century humanism. The views are dramatic and the crossing is full of excitement. After the aqueduct comes a tunnel, a long wooded cutting and then another tunnel, which leaves the canal high on the side of the broad valley of the Dee. At first it clings desperately to the hillside, with wonderful views spread out below, and then it takes cover again in the woodland. It turns towards the valley on a high embankment, still hiding among the trees. The next moment is pure theatre, and there is nothing to match it anywhere in Britain. As your boat leaves the shelter of the trees, it is suddenly in the air, apparently flying across the valley of the Dee on a thin ribbon of water. The river is 120ft below, and the views are breathtaking. This is Telford's great Pontcysyllte aqueduct, a narrow iron trough carried for 1,000ft across the valley on a series of tall stone piers. It was completed in 1805 and has astonished spectators ever since. When he presented his plans, they were greeted with the derision that normally

accompanies any new brilliant idea. No one believed it would work, and yet today this masterpiece still stands, as good as the day it was completed. Crossing it is an extraordinary experience. The illusion of flying is strong because, while there is a balustraded towpath on one side, on the other there is absolutely nothing, just the top of the iron trough a few inches above the water line. Standing on the deck of a boat you are, apparently, in thin air, with nothing between you and the river far below. I have crossed it many times, by boat, on foot, and even on a bicycle, and the pure excitement never diminishes. It has to be the greatest canal thrill in Britain, and maybe the world, but anyone with a fear of heights should stay firmly below. Even the towing horses had to be blinkered, and especially trained, before they would venture across.

At the other end is a short arm leading to Ruabon, a town famous for its bricks, tiles and terracotta. The immediate temptation is to turn round here and do it again. This arm is actually all that was built of the Ellesmere Company's canal northwards from here to Chester.

Before the arm, there is a junction with a narrow little canal, a sharp turn into something that looks almost too small for boats. This is the navigable feeder to Llantisilio, the final act of the Llangollen drama. This is a spectacular journey with the canal following the Dee Valley, its route in and out of the trees high on the side of the hill, and in places it barely clings to a precipitous slope. It is narrow, with few places for boats to pass, and always the views are extraordinary. A boat seems, after all, the least suitable vehicle imaginable for a journey through the mountains, and yet the Llangollen Canal brings this fantasy to life.

Llangollen itself, set on the tumbling waters of the Dee, is spread far below the canal. Apart from its well-known charms, and its annual International Eisteddfod, Llangollen also offers visitors a canal museum and a steam railway that runs along a fine stretch of the Dee Valley on a restored section of what must have been one of the best of Britain's scenic lines. There is no turning point for boats beyond Llangollen, so most people walk the final stretch to Llantisilio, to admire Telford's Horseshoe Falls, a picturesque semi-circular weir built to capture the waters of the Dee and send them down the canal to England. Towering over the canal are

the rocky remains of Castell Dinas Bran, the great fortress built high on its 1,100ft mountain crest by Eliseg, Prince of Powys, with the express purpose of keeping the English out. Centuries later, the English are still invading Wales, but many now come by canal boat, generally with friendly intentions. Today the Welsh shelter behind their impenetrable language rather than mountain fortresses, but even they have to acknowledge that the appeal of the Llangollen is universal, and international.

Above: *Horseshoe Falls near Llantisilio, the end of the Llangollen Canal, and its feeder from the River Dee.*

PLACES TO VISIT

Chirk: Castle, a late 13th-century Marcher fortress, complete with drum towers, portcullis and dungeon; occupied for 700 years, it has a 17th-century Long Gallery, elegant staterooms noted for their delicate 18th-century plasterwork, and 19th-century work by A W N Pugin; fine tapestries, portraits and furniture; landscaped park with intricate wrought iron gates (National Trust).

Cole Mere Country Park, on the south side of the canal, 3 miles SE of Ellesmere: waymarked walks circle the lake, passing through woodland and flowery meadows.

Llangollen: Horse Drawn Boats and Canal Exhibition Centre, imaginative and informative museum with working and static models; horsedrawn boat trips, plus narrow boat trip over Pontcysyllte aqueduct.

Llangollen Railway: steam and diesel 10½-mile round trips through the Dee Valley between Llangollen's restored GWR station and Glyndyfrdwy.

Plas Newydd Museum: where the 'Ladies of Llangollen', Lady Eleanor Butler and Sarah Ponsonby, set up house, entertaining such distinguished visitors as Wordsworth, Shelley and the Duke of Wellington; a curious black and white house full of personal bits and pieces.

Valle Crucis Abbey: substantial and attractive ruins of a Cistercian abbey founded in 1201 on a wooded slope above Eglwyseg River (now in the care of Cadw).

Offa's Dyke Path: the national trail that for the most part follows the 8th-century earthwork may be joined near Pontcysyllte aqueduct.

Stapeley Water Gardens, 1 mile S of Nantwich: national collection of over 100 varieties of water lily, 50 acres of lakes, pools and fountains, plus the Palms Tropical Oasis with sharks, piranhas, giant Amazon lilies.

Sun Bank, 1½ miles E of Llangollen: Sun Trevor, beautifully situated, ancient canalside pub with wonderful views of the canal, the Dee and the wooded hills behind.

The Caledonian Canal

*I*T WAS a clear Sunday morning but the streets of Inverness were still empty when I left the station. I had travelled up on the overnight train from London and, my hunger stimulated by British Rail's early morning tea and biscuits, I was now looking forward to breakfast. I knew it was going to be a good one, but first I had to find it. A few days before, the captain had told me to look for the ship in the basin below Muirtown locks and so, not wanting to miss the boat, and not knowing Inverness very well, I took a taxi. It was a short journey through the town and across the River Ness. As the basin came into view there was no mistaking the ship. Sitting at the quay was a large, black and workmanlike vessel, with a tall red funnel set towards the stern. Smoke and steam rose slowly towards the sky. Immediately behind the funnel was the bridge, a tall timber structure, glazed all round, and looking like a cross between a signal box and a greenhouse. This rather curious parentage was confirmed by the presence of some very large tomato plants pressing their leaves and fruit against the windows. I sent the taxi away and walked down the quay, savouring not only my first sight of a steam puffer, the classic ship of the Clyde and the Western Highlands, but also the delicious aroma of breakfast that wafted through the still air. The oily, smoky smells of a steam engine are alluring enough but, when mixed with a hint of toast, bacon and coffee, they are completely irresistible. It is a pity perfume-makers do not pay more attention to the smells that really turn men on, for any girl wearing this exotic blend of tempting scents would never be short of admirers.

The view of Ben Nevis from Banavie.

The Caledonian Canal

From Clachnaharry on the Beauly Firth, near
Inverness, to Corpach near Fort William
60 miles long, with 29 broad locks
The canal incorporates in its route four natural
lochs, Dochfour, Ness, Oich and Lochy.

Notable features Clachnaharry and the entry to
Beauly Firth, Muirtown locks in Inverness, Loch
Ness and Urquhart Castle, Fort Augustus, Loch
Oich and Invergarry Castle, Laggan Cutting and
locks, Loch Lochy, Gairlochy locks, Banavie locks
(Neptune's Staircase) and railway swing bridge,
Corpach basin and locks.

History The original plan for a waterway to link
the east and west coasts of Scotland via the Great
Glen was drawn up in 1773 by James Watt, but it
was Thomas Telford who masterminded the
actual building of the canal between 1803 and
1822. From the start it was massively supported
by the government, keen to help the local fishing
industry, to provide vessels with a safer
alternative to the hazardous Pentland Firth and to
give employment to local people and thus stop
the flow of emigration that had followed the
Highland Clearances. Despite having continuous
government grants, the canal cost over three
times Telford's original budget, and even when
completed it remained in deficit, the yearly
income rarely matching expenditure. The
difficulties of the terrain and the demanding
nature of the engineering meant that the canal
had to be extensively rebuilt during the 1830s and
1840s. A mixture of fishing boats, passenger
vessels and some cargo carriers travelled on the
canal, but there were never many more than 1,000
users per year. From quite an early date, the
Caledonian attracted the interest of visitors, keen
to admire the blend of spectacular scenery and
dramatic engineering, and pleasure usage has
always been important. Although a financial
liability, and a white elephant in commercial
terms, the Caledonian has never been without
government support, mainly for political and
social reasons, and as a result it has at no point
been a serious candidate for closure. Today, its
contribution to the leisure industry of the
Highlands is increasingly valuable. At the same
time, it is unique among British waterways in
terms of both scale and setting.

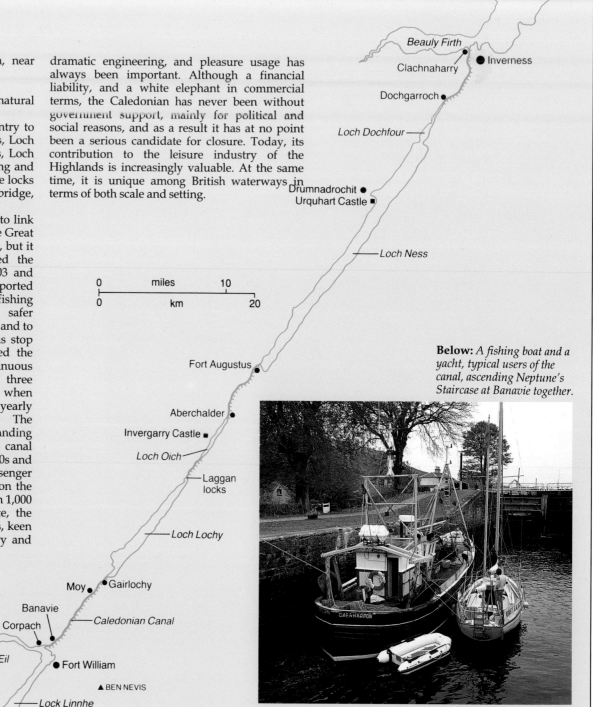

Below: *A fishing boat and a
yacht, typical users of the
canal, ascending Neptune's
Staircase at Banavie together.*

I climbed on board and went below, to be greeted by the captain, who was seated at the head of a long table, presiding over the most magnificent breakfast. There was everything, from porridge and kippers to freshly baked breads and home-made marmalade, via oatcakes, bacon and local cheeses. Tucking into this feast, I learned about the orders for the day. When breakfast was over, and steam was raised, we would set off up the Muirhead locks, the first stage of our progress along the Caledonian Canal. First, there was time for a stroll round the basin and a leisurely examination of the swing bridge that carries the railway to Wick and Thurso across the canal. The Caledonian actually starts at Clachnaharry, its entrance from the Beauly Firth marked by a sea lock at the end of a stretch of embankment that keeps the canal apart from the tidal waters of the estuary.

Some time later, amid much hooting, ringing of bells, shouting and general mayhem, we did finally cast off, and the ship moved away from the quay, a dense cloud of black smoke indicating that some serious shovelling of coal was going on down below in the engine room. Most of the passengers and crew remained on shore, to walk up the locks, give a hand with the odd rope or two, and

Above: *The embankment at Clachnaharry that carries the canal out into the Beauly Firth.*

Left: *Scotrail bridge keeper at Clachnaharry, operating the swing bridge across the canal.*

generally admire the bluff lines and high bow of this tough traditional workhorse, one of the last survivors of the once great fleet of puffers that for decades had kept the Scottish islands supplied with all their needs, from tractors to toothbrushes. There are four locks at Muirtown, built as a staircase, and then the canal, skirting the western suburbs of Inverness but offering good views of the town's churches and castle, follows closely the winding course of the Ness to Dochgarroch, where a single lock raises it to the level of Loch Dochfour. This is the smallest of the four lochs incorporated into the Caledonian's route and, as canal, river and loch all merge together, the scene is set for the most splendid inland waterway journey in Britain.

After a couple of miles, Loch Dochfour narrows to its southern end. Ahead lie the waters of the far mightier Loch Ness, the entrance to the loch being marked by a lighthouse, a rather rare waterway

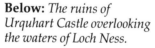

Left: *Washing at Dochgarroch lock - taking advantage of the canal's easy passage to catch up with domestic chores.*

Below: *The ruins of Urquhart Castle overlooking the waters of Loch Ness.*

sight. Twenty three miles long, about a mile wide, up to 700ft deep, and traditionally populated by monsters, Loch Ness is too well known to require much introduction. We steamed along the loch that day in beautiful sunshine, across a surface of deep blue slightly ruffled by gusts of wind, sailing most of the time close to the western shore to enjoy better the landscape of steep woods and distant mountains. Various passengers, including myself, took turns at the wheel, and so we steered a somewhat erratic course whose meanderings kept us safe from both submarines and monsters. In fact even the most seaworthy among us found it hard to keep the ship on an even course, for the view ahead from the wheelhouse was severely limited by the great bulk of the funnel and the tomato plants. The helmsman had to spend much of the period of duty leaning out of the side windows which rather endearingly went up and down on leather thongs, like those in very old railway carriages. We steamed steadily on, our progress marked by occasional clouds of black smoke as the amateur stokers did their worst down below, and then we anchored for lunch in Urquhart Bay, below the remains of the great castle. After another magnificent feast shore leave was granted for those wishing to take the

ship's boat to visit the castle, ruined before the Jacobite rebellions of the early 18th century.

And so the afternoon passed. Later, with everyone back on board, and the boat back in its place on top of the hold thanks to the efforts of the steam winch, we sailed slowly on while tea was served and then, as the light was beginning to go, we came to Fort Augustus, the end of our passage along Loch Ness marked by another lighthouse. Back in a canal again, we moored for the night at the foot of the five staircase locks, happy to leave that labour for the next day.

Fort Augustus proved, on inspection, to be a quiet place, a few houses and shops and General Wade's fort, named after William Augustus, Duke of Cumberland, which is now an abbey and monastery maintained by the Benedictines. The canal runs through the heart of Fort Augustus and it must, in the days when boats were travelling regularly up and down the lochs, have been a busy waterway town. It even had a railway station, the end of a branch line closed years ago. Having done the town, so to speak, we returned on board, ready

for the next gastronomic creation to emerge from the tiny galley. Then, soothed by some delectable malts and the soft tones of Ambrose played on the ship's steam-powered gramophone, we retired to our quarters.

The next morning I had to abandon ship rather early, to return to Inverness and then to London by the nine o'clock train. Leaving passengers and crew slumbering, and the puffer gently at rest, smoke drifting from the funnel, I walked down to the main road, bracing myself for the unwelcome task of hitching a lift, something not attempted for years. Luckily my hesitantly raised thumb attracted the attention of the first lorry to pass, and I was able to reverse in an hour along the loch-side road the journey that had taken all the previous day. Sitting on the train and enjoying the view, I envied my fellow passengers their journey along the rest of the canal, knowing that any further explorations of the Caledonian would have to wait until another day.

It is without doubt the most remarkable and the most spectacular waterway in Britain, seen at its best from a boat as parts are inaccessible by road. The Caledonian canal has a complex background, and its story is as extraordinary as its continued presence in the heart of the Highlands.

The idea of an artificial waterway to link the west and east coasts of Scotland goes back to the early 18th century, but the first practical proposal was that prepared by James Watt in 1773. The inspiration was twofold, first to enable vessels to avoid the dangerous waters of the Pentland Firth, and second, to help the fishing industry by connecting the east and west coast fishing grounds. Watt surveyed a route from Fort William to Inverness via Lochs Lochy, Oich, Ness and Dochfour, a natural choice following the line of the Great Glen across the country, and one that was also recommended by Thomas Telford when, 30 years later, he was asked by the government to reconsider the problem. By this time, two other factors supported the idea of the canal, the need to protect ships from French privateers and the hope

that it would reverse the flow of emigration from the Highlands. Telford, always a man of great foresight, believed that the building of the canal, as a vital part of the infrastructure of the region, would not only give employment to thousands but would also encourage the development of industry. He reported that a waterway 60 miles long and 20ft deep, with 28 large locks 170ft by 40ft, could be built in seven years for £350,000. As always, this proved to be a wildly inaccurate estimate of the costs. In 1803 the government gave £20,000 towards the project, starting the principle of public support for the Caledonian that has continued to the present day. A board of commissioners was appointed to manage it, and Telford was given the job of principal engineer, with William Jessop as his assistant. In 1804 the government gave a second grant, of £50,000, and work started at the eastern and western ends. Despite a huge labour force,

Above: *Working yachts down Fort Augustus locks, and taking a tea break.*

Opposite: *Naval training ship steaming through the Laggan cutting.*

progress was slow, and the costs mounted steadily. By 1811 under half of the canal was complete, and £343,000 had been spent. Problems were compounded by the difficulties of the terrain, the weather, and by a workforce that was in no hurry to complete what they knew to be little more than a giant job creation scheme. The government continued to pour money into the canal, the annual grant of £50,000 often having to be increased. As technology improved, so new and expensive machinery was brought into use. Steam power was widely used and the laborious task of deepening Loch Oich was carried out by two of the first steam bucket dredgers in the world. With the ending of the Napoleonic wars, one of the canal's primary *raisons d'être* disappeared, and many began to believe the whole thing should be abandoned. However, work continued, mainly on the basis of the social value and political stability maintained by the levels of employment. By 1818 the costs had reached £700,000, but the work, and the grants, continued, and in October 1822 the Caledonian Canal was formally opened, having cost over £905,000.

In the 12 months from May 1823, 844 vessels used the canal, carrying passengers and a variety of cargoes, and the average time taken for the whole journey was between three and four days. This pattern continued through the 1820s, but already problems were becoming apparent. Revenues were well below expectations, and so income was not enough to maintain the canal, let alone repay any of the accrued debts. Indeed, throughout the canal's working life there were to be few years when revenue exceeded expenditure. Worse still were the structural defects in the locks. As early as 1826 one, at Gairlochy, had collapsed and had to be extensively repaired. Others followed, notably in the flights at Fort Augustus and Banavie, and so during the 1830s and 1840s the canal was, in effect, completely rebuilt at enormous cost, and with major contributions from the government. On 1st

Below: *Neptune's Staircase at Banavie, the canal's most ambitious engineering feature.*

May 1847 it was reopened throughout to traffic, having been dredged to 17ft, and equipped with a fleet of four steam tugs to encourage traffic. Despite all these improvements, the level of use remained much the same, and through the 19th century the canal continued to be a drain on public resources. The Caledonian was, none the less, a success in the eyes of the public. It was widely seen as a triumph of modern engineering, and its magnificence was celebrated in prose and poetry, notably by Robert Southey. From the 1850s it became an essential sight for visitors to the Highlands, and in 1873 Queen Victoria travelled the whole length of the canal on the steamboat *Gondolier*.

At the end of the 19th century there were various schemes to rebuild the Caledonian with larger locks, in the hope of stimulating trade, but these all came to nothing, and the primary users remained fishing boats taking a short cut across the Scottish mainland. This, at least, fulfilled one of the original justifications for the canal. Another, the encouragement of industry, finally came to life in this century with the development of an aluminium plant and a paper mill, resulting in a massive enlargement of the terminal basin at Corpach, at the Fort William end. These had little effect on the canal itself, and traffic levels were largely unaltered. In fact, the only time the Caledonian has been genuinely busy was during the two World Wars, when smaller naval vessels made great use of it as a link between east and west coast bases.

Commenting on the canal's centenary in 1922, the *Glasgow Herald* doubted if it had ever justified its huge costs. Despite this widespread point of view it remained in use, operated initially by the Ministry of Transport, later the British Transport Commission and then by the British Waterways Board, who took it over in 1962. Apart from a programme of lock mechanisation, the canal has since been largely unchanged and the number of users, now mostly fishing boats and pleasure craft, is no greater than it was a century ago.

The Caledonian remains a wonderful folly, a

classic white elephant, and a delightful way to see the spectacular scenery of the Highlands. And it was this aspect that first drew me to it. Commissioned many years ago to write about the west coast of Scotland, I came by stages to Fort William along the shore of Loch Linnhe. My taste for Scotland's canals had already been stimulated by an exploration of the Crinan, further south, and the Caledonian proved to be irresistible, although not strictly on my route. I started at Corpach, looking at the ships serving the pulp mill, and drawn particularly by the old swing bridge that carries the railway to Mallaig over the canal.

Above: *Fishing boat leaving Corpach double lock.*

Attractively archaic, it makes the modern road swing bridge alongside positively boring. There is a fine old station, Banavie, by the bridge, setting the scene for one of the best train journeys in Britain. I have done it a number of times, but the one that sticks in the mind is a steam-hauled trip through the worst of Scotland's rain and mist, the pounding of the locomotive and its echoing whistle easily making up for the invisible scenery. On my first visit it was very different, with all the golden colours of a Scottish autumn throwing Ben Nevis into high relief above Fort William. From Corpach I walked up to Banavie to look at the famous flight of eight locks, known, not surprisingly, as Neptune's Staircase, which lifts the canal 64ft. It is certainly an extraordinary sight, unlike anything else in Britain, and its grandeur underlines the impressive scale of Telford's engineering. From the top of the Banavie flight there is about 7 miles of canal, running beside the River Lochy all the way to Loch Lochy. The setting is magnificent, with the bulk of Ben Nevis filling the horizon to the southeast. At Gairlochy there are two further locks and a swing bridge, and

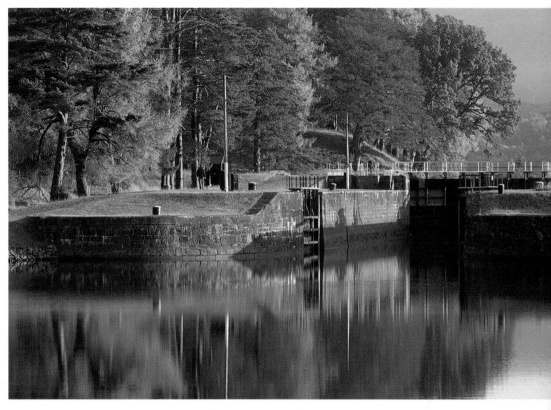

Above: *Autumn colours at Gairlochy locks.*

Left: *Fishing boat at Gairlochy.*

Opposite: *Ben Nevis, shrouded in cloud, stands guard over Fort William and the canal near Corpach.*

then the canal joins Loch Lochy with another lighthouse to mark the spot. Loch Lochy is deep and its wooded shores fall steeply into the water. Along the eastern water's edge can be seen the route of the former branch line to Fort Augustus, one of the many exciting railway journeys in Scotland sacrificed to rationalisation. It is actually remarkable that the Mallaig line has survived, and one should be grateful at least that it was spared.

The canal leaves Loch Lochy at its northern end and then climbs at once the two Laggan locks, which raise it to its summit level. There is another swing bridge and from here a short stretch of tree-lined canal set in a spectacular cutting crosses the Highland watershed to connect Lochs Lochy and Oich. Loch Oich, unlike the others on the route, is shallow, and the dredged channel along it is marked by buoys and lights. It needs in any case to be taken slowly to make the most of its exciting scenery. Halfway along, on the western side, are the ruins of Invergarry Castle, destroyed, like so many, by the Duke of Cumberland after Culloden. At the head of the loch a swing bridge marks the start of the final stretch of canal, a 5-mile section that links Loch Oich to Fort Augustus. This is particularly remote, with no real road access, and so has to be

seen by boat or on foot. Two isolated locks, set in the middle of nowhere, start the canal's descent towards Inverness. During that first visit I did not go beyond Fort Augustus, for my west coast tour had the kind of impossible schedule that seems to be endemic to guide book research. The whole of the west coast, from the Solway Firth to Cape Wrath, and a few islands thrown in for good measure, had to be covered in two weeks, and in sufficient depth to write about it in a useful and accurate manner. We achieved it by using every second of available daylight, by sleeping when we stopped in the old van being used as a research vehicle – there being, as usual, a tiny budget – and by driving interminably along hundreds of miles of the narrow tracks that in those days passed for roads in the Highlands. I remember falling asleep at the wheel only once, and we drifted gently into a roadside ditch, from which we were rescued, undamaged, by passers by. Having succumbed to the lure of the Caledonian, I had put us behind schedule, and so it was back to Fort William and then off along the northern shore of Loch Linnhe. To be able, years later, to complete my tour of the Caledonian Canal in style and at leisure on a steam puffer was more than adequate compensation.

Opposite: Looking southeast through Laggan cutting, between Loch Lochy and Loch Oich.

PLACES TO VISIT

Castle Stuart, 5 miles NE of Inverness: built in 1621, when the Stuarts ruled the United Kingdom; home of the Earls of Moray and the Stuart family, Jacobean furnishings, armour.
Clava Cairns, 6 miles E of Inverness: a group of three circular burial cairns ringed by standing stones.
Corpach: Treasures of the Earth, an outstanding collection of crystals, gemstones and fossils, including the biggest uncut emerald in the world, displayed in a re-creation of underground caves and mines.
Culloden Battlefield, 5 miles E of Inverness: a National Trust for Scotland visitor centre on the moorland site of the 1746 battle, the last fought on mainland Britain and the end of the Jacobite Rising.
Drumnadrochit: Official Loch Ness Monster

Exhibition, computer-controlled, multi-media presentation tells the story from pre-history onwards.
Urquhart Castle, overlooks Loch Ness, once one of the largest castles in Scotland, dating partly from Norman times, blown up at the end of the 17th century to prevent occupation by the Jacobites (Historic Scotland).
Divach Falls, approximately 1½-mile walk from Lewiston, cascade 100ft down a rocky valley of oak and birch.
Farigaig Forest Centre: woodland walks, interpretive centre.
Fort Augustus: St Benedict's Abbey, founded in 1867 and incorporating part of a Hanoverian fort built by General Wade in 1730.
Lock Inn, cosy and atmospheric, right beside the canal.
Fort William: Ben Nevis Distillery, 1½ miles N,

offers guided tours with a free dram at the end.
The Gondola, ride 2,150ft up the steep slopes of Aonach Mor.
West Highland Museum has exhibits on traditional crofting life, plenty of Jacobite relics and a secret portrait of Bonnie Prince Charlie.
West Highland Way long-distance footpath runs 95 miles south to the outskirts of Glasgow.
Inverness: Art Gallery & Museum for bagpipes, Jacobite relics and more. Balnain House, a restored Georgian house overlooking the Ness, home to Scotland's Highland Music Museum.
Balnain House, a restored Georgian house overlooking the Ness, home to Scotland's Highland Music Museum.
St Andrew's Cathedral, a richly decorated late 19th-century building.
Spean Bridge, 2 miles E of Gairlochy: Commando Memorial and Museum, commemorates the

CANALS AND NAVIGABLE WATERWAYS
OF ENGLAND AND WALES

Ripon Canal
Lancaster Canal
Leeds & Liverpool Canal
River Ouse
River Derwent
Aire & Calder Canal
Pocklington Canal
Preston
Leeds
Rochdale Canal
Huddersfield Broad Canal
Huddersfield Narrow Canal
Sheffield & South Yorkshire Navigation
Manchester Ship Canal
Manchester
Peak Forest Canal
Sheffield
Liverpool
Bridgewater Canal
Fossdyke & Witham Navigation
Ellesmere Port
Macclesfield Canal
Chesterfield Canal
Lincoln
Chester
Caldon Canal
Cromford Canal
Trent & Mersey Canal
River Trent
Boston
Stoke-on-Trent
Nottingham Canal
Llangollen
Erewash Canal
Nottingham
River Welland
Llangollen Canal
Derby Canal
River Ant
Shropshire Union Canal
Trent & Mersey Canal
Grantham Canal
River Bure
River Thurne
Montgomery Canal
Coventry Canal
Grand Union Canal (Leicester section)
River Nene
Norwich
Great Y
Leicester
River Great Ouse
Birmingham Canal Navigations
River Yare
Ashby Canal
Little Ouse
River Waveney
Staffordshire & Worcestershire Canal
Birmingham
Oxford Canal
New Bedford River
River Lark
Stratford-on-Avon Canal
River Cam
Worcester & Birmingham Canal
Northampton
Cambridge
Worcester
Stratford
River Avon
River Severn
Brecon
Monmouthshire & Brecon Canal
Grand Union Canal
Gloucester & Sharpness Canal
Gloucester
Oxford Canal
River Stort
Stroudwater Canal
Aylesbury
North Wilts Canal
Oxford
River Lee
Thames & Severn Canal
Regents Canal
Newport
River Thames
London
Glamorganshire Canal
Wilts & Berks Canal
Bristol
Reading
Bath
Maidstone
River Avon
River Wey
River Medway
Kennet & Avon Canal
Basingstoke Canal
Bridgwater & Taunton Canal
River Parrett
Wey & Arun Canal
River Arun
Royal Military Canal
Torrington Canal
Taunton
River Tone
Portsmouth & Arundel Canal
River Rother
Chard Canal
Rye
Bude
Grand Western Canal
Portsmouth
Bude Canal
Exeter
Exeter Ship Canal
Launceston

KEY

——— Navigable canals

- - - - Disused or partly restored canals

——— Navigable rivers

0   miles   50
0   km   100

Inverness

Loch Ness

Caledonian Canal

Loch Lochy

Fort William

Crinan
Canal

Forth & Clyde
Canal

Firth
of Forth

Edinburgh

Glasgow

Edinburgh & Glasgow Union Canal

River
Clyde

A Gazetteer
of Britain's Canals

*B*RITAIN still has over 2,000 miles of navigable inland waterways, widely spread over most parts of the country and usually interconnected. As a result, there are very few cities in Britain that do not have a waterway of some kind that is capable of carrying boats. Much of this mileage is, of course, made up from the major river navigations, for example the Thames, the Medway, the Severn, the Trent, the Humber, the Nene, the Warwickshire Avon, the Yorkshire Ouse and so on, waterways that are outside the scope of this book. Many canals follow routes which, for obvious reasons, their engineers based upon existing rivers and streams, but there is a distinction to be drawn between natural water courses made navigable and artificial canals built from scratch where no significant navigation previously existed. By and large, canals are easier to explore than rivers. They are readily accessible from bridges and locks, and they always have towpaths, which, when in good repair, make excellent footpaths. On most active canals, in the care of British Waterways, there is a right of way along the towpath. This may not apply to some privately owned canals and rarely applies to canals that have been officially abandoned. Exploring forgotten canals can be very enjoyable, but it is necessary always to bear in mind rules governing access and trespass. Equally, there is rarely any public right of access to the private, that is to say the non-towpath, side of a canal.

Listed on the following pages is a selection of British canals, both used and disused, that are worth exploring. The exploration can range from a short afternoon's walk to a real long-distance hike. In either case, it is essential to carry the relevant Ordnance Survey map. Also useful are the Nicholson series of waterway guides, although these are aimed primarily at the canal boater and so show only a narrow strip of country either side of the canal. There are, of course, many more canals in Britain than those listed here. Useful sources of reference for these and other inland waterways are:

De Salis, Henry, *Bradshaw's Canals and Navigable Rivers of England and Wales*, (1904, reprinted 1969)
Edwards, L A, *Inland Waterways of Great Britain*
McKnight, Hugh, *The Shell Book of Inland Waterways*
Rolt, L C T, *The Inland Waterways of England*
Rolt, L C T, *Narrow Boat*
Russell, Ronald, *Lost Canals of England and Wales*

THE SOUTH OF ENGLAND

The Basingstoke Canal and the Wey and Arun Canal

The River Wey, one of the earliest river navigations in Britain to be built with locks, is an attractive waterway that connects the Thames with two other canals. The Wey itself, opened from Weybridge to Guildford in 1653, and then later extended to Godalming, is today used and operated by the National Trust. At West Byfleet there is a junction with the Basingstoke Canal, recently restored after several decades of dereliction and confused ownership. With its surprisingly rural nature and wooded surroundings, its 29 locks and its interesting engineering features, which include a deep cutting at Mytchett and an impressive aqueduct over the main railway line from Waterloo to southern and western England, it is a canal whose restoration has

Above: *The Basingstoke Canal at North Warnborough, Hampshire.*

been long overdue. The 31-mile route now ends at the 1,200yd Greywell Tunnel, whose collapse was one of the factors that prompted the canal's closure. Originally it continued to Basingstoke, but much of the route west of the tunnel has been obliterated. During its years of dereliction, the Basingstoke had become a kind of unofficial nature reserve, and since its restoration there has been some conflict between wildlife and boating interests. As a result, powered craft are forbidden on the canal's upper reaches, making it particularly attractive for walkers.

The Wey's other connection is with the remains of another of the great failures of the canal age. An ambitious early 19th-century

Left: *The Wey & Arun Canal at Dunsford.*

scheme was for a waterway from London to the south coast, and the Wey & Arun Canal, opened in 1816, was a vital link in the complex route to Portsmouth that involved the Thames, the Wey, the Arun, and Portsmouth Harbour. Notably unsuccessful, the canal never carried more than 3,600 tons per year, and it proved a very poor investment for Lord Egremont and its other promoters. It finally closed in 1871, by which time the Portsmouth Harbour sections had already been abandoned. Unspectacular in engineering terms, the Wey & Arun wanders through the quiet countryside of Surrey and Sussex, with only the 23 locks to show that it ever was a canal. For many years it was a truly lost canal, but since the 1970s a programme of restoration has been under way and in the future it may be possible for boats again to leave the Wey at Shalford and meander southwards to meet the Arun Navigation at Newbridge. More restoration work will be required here, for the Arun itself has been inaccessible to boats above its tidal head at Pallingham for a century. The reopening of the whole route is unlikely. The best way to see the Wey & Arun is on foot; it makes a very enjoyable weekend walk.

The Bridgwater and Taunton Canal and its connections

One of the greatest of the unfulfilled schemes of the canal age was the building of a waterway to link Bristol and Exeter. There were various late 18th- and early 19th-century proposals and, although the through route remained a dream, a number of canals were built as independent parts of it. One such was the Bridgwater & Taunton, a 14-mile waterway that took nearly 20 years to construct. Finally completed in 1841, the canal, originally conceived as part of a much larger Bristol to Taunton waterway, was in the end little better than a more convenient alternative to the existing Tone and Parrett river navigations that linked Bridgwater with

Above: *Horsedrawn boat on the Grand Western Canal, Tiverton, Devon.*

Taunton. Its most successful feature was the dock complex at Bridgwater, a busy coal port from the 1840s whose basins were often filled with trading schooners. The docks, in use until the 1960s, long outlived the canal which was disused by the early 20th century, having been in railway ownership since 1866. Long closed, the canal has recently been restored, but it has lost all its former connections. Apart from the Parrett and Tone navigations, these included the Chard Canal, one of the least successful of all Britain's waterways. Its 13½ mile route from Creech St Michael to Chard was expensive and heavily engineered, with three tunnels, two aqueducts and four inclined planes. Opened in 1842, it was closed by 1867, having been a total loss for its promoters, but surprisingly much of its route can still be traced and its major engineering features identified and explored. The other

connection was with the extravagantly named Grand Western Canal, planned in the late 18th century by John Rennie as a waterway link between the Exe and the Tone, and with three branches. In 1816 the branch to Tiverton was opened and in 1838 this was finally extended to Taunton. No more of the Grand Western was ever built and those parts that were completed had been overtaken by railways within ten years. The Tiverton to Loudwells section survived, unexpectedly, and has recently been restored. The route from Loudwells to Taunton, with its dramatic boat lifts and inclined planes, was abandoned decades ago, but plenty of traces remain.

The Bude Canal

The needs of agriculture inspired the construction of many canals, particularly in western England, for sea sand was widely

Above: *Entrance into the canal at Bude Harbour, Cornwall.*

used as a fertiliser. The primary example is the Bude Canal, a 35-mile network of waterways completed in 1825 to transport sand from Bude to the villages and farms around Holsworthy and the Tamar. It was built as a tub-boat canal, and its main feature was the series of inclined planes, mostly operated by water wheels. The tub-boats, small square barges, were hauled by horses in trains of up to six, and they were fitted with wheels to allow them to be drawn up the inclined planes on rails. Reasonably successful, the network remained in use at least until the 1880s, when the railways took away the trade. Plenty of the route can still be traced, and the sites of the inclined planes can be explored. At the Bude end there is still a sea lock and an enclosed basin, the start of two miles of barge canal. Also to be seen are the tracks of the old railways leading from the

basin to the beach. The sand was loaded into horse-drawn wagons and carried to the barges lying in the basin. These transported it to the start of the narrow tub-boat network where, transhipped into the tubs, it began its tortuous journey into the hinterland. With plenty still visible on the ground, the Bude Canal offers a valuable insight into an entirely forgotten way of life.

The Exeter Ship Canal

Opened in its original form in 1566, this was the first canal in Britain to be built with locks. It was subsequently enlarged and rebuilt, in 1701 and 1830, to become a 5-mile waterway linking Exeter Docks with the sea via the estuary of the Exe, capable of handling boats up to 400 tons. Its main features are the 19th-century warehouses in Exeter, now housing the Maritime Museum, and its

attractive route beside the Exe, via Topsham. The canal's final lock, Turf, was built in 1830 to allow vessels drawing up to 12ft to enter the canal at any state of the tide.

The Gloucester and Sharpness Canal

At the time of its opening in 1827, this was the largest ship canal in the world, a major waterway built to bypass a particularly treacherous and unpredictable stretch of the River Severn. Work on it had begun in 1793, but the large size, and the great costs involved, continuously delayed construction, and it was only finished with large sums of government money, granted to alleviate chronic local unemployment. However, its scale, its ship size locks and its movable bridges allowing unlimited headroom have ensured its commercial survival to the present day. It runs for 16¾ miles from Gloucester Docks to Sharpness Docks with a connection to the Severn at each end, and it is these dock complexes that are its greatest attraction today. Gloucester Docks, a complex of basins surrounded by fine 19th-century warehouses, is now given over largely to pleasure traffic, and is the home of the National Waterways Museum. Sharpness, by comparison, is still a busy inland dock area, full of interest. Along its route the canal passes the Wildfowl and Wetlands Trust Centre at Slimbridge, and Saul Junction, a canal crossroads where the derelict Stroudwater crossed the Gloucester & Sharpness. Until its closure, the Stroudwater linked with the Thames & Severn Canal, providing a direct waterway connection between the two rivers.

The Oxford Canal

One of the first of Britain's trunk route canals, and the first link, via the Thames, between London and the industrial centres of the Midlands, the Oxford Canal was authorised

Right: *Restored warehouses at Gloucester docks, on the Gloucester & Sharpness Canal.*

in 1769. It was to connect the new Coventry Canal with Oxford via Banbury, and its inspiration was the carriage of coal southwards from Warwickshire to London. James Brindley was its first engineer, and he planned a very meandering 91-mile route in order to keep costs down. He died in 1772, but construction continued to his plans, and the canal reached Banbury in 1778. There was then a long delay, and it was not finally opened to Oxford until 1790. Not long after, the opening of the more direct Grand Junction Canal took much of the Oxford's trade, and so in the 1820s much of its route was rebuilt, with many of the old twists and turns replaced by straight lines, embankments and cuttings. Between Braunston and the Coventry Canal the original 36-mile route was shortened by 14 miles. Little was done to the southern section, but trade survived, and the Oxford was still carrying coal in the early 1960s. Today, its wandering route, old brick bridges and attractive narrow locks add greatly to its appeal, for the Oxford still has something of the feel of an 18th-century waterway about it.

Above: *Manoeuvring boats at Brinklow on the Oxford Canal.*

The Royal Military Canal
In the far southeastern corner of England there is one of Britain's most unusual waterways. As its name implies, the Royal Military Canal was conceived and built entirely for defensive purposes, inspired by the fear of invasion by Napoleonic forces on the Kentish marshes. It was built between 1804 and 1806 and its route runs from Shorncliffe near Hythe to the River Rother at Iden, near Rye, and then south from Rye to Winchelsea and Cliff End, a total of 30 miles. It was planned both for the movement of troops and gunboats, and as a line of defence to hold the invading forces at bay, but by the time the canal was completed, the invasion threat had largely disappeared and so its owners, the government, while retaining their military interest in the waterway, turned it

over to commercial use. Commercial traffic, mostly carrying building materials, then continued for about a century. Since then, the canal has quietly declined, but the whole route survives, to be explored and enjoyed by anyone with an interest in military history, and an enthusiasm for the distinctive landscape of the Romney Marshes.

The Stratford-on-Avon Canal
Famous as the first canal in Britain to be rescued from closure and obliteration by public protest, and then restored by voluntary labour, the Stratford-on-Avon is an attractive waterway built to link Stratford to the canal network, and thus provide an alternative route from the Severn to Birmingham via the Avon Navigation. Its 25-mile route, with 54

narrow locks, was slow and expensive to build. Started in 1793, it was not completed until 1816, and its commercial life was relatively short. Bought by the Great Western Railway in 1856, it then declined steadily until its southern section, from the junction with the Grand Union at Lapworth to Stratford, was virtually derelict by the 1930s. The northern section, from Lapworth to King's Norton, where it joined the Worcester & Birmingham Canal for the journey into Birmingham, remained in occasional use. Now a popular cruising waterway, the Stratford-on-Avon has many appealing features, particularly its rural route, its aqueducts, its barrel-roofed lock cottages and its cast iron bridges, split to allow the passage of the towing rope.

Above: *'Guillotine' bridge at Lapworth on the Stratford-on-Avon Canal.*

The Torrington Canal

Privately financed by the Rolle family, the Torrington Canal was opened in 1827 to transport sand and lime from the estuary of the River Torridge, near Bideford, 6 miles inland to Torrington, and to serve the farms along the way. It was closed in 1871 and much of it quickly disappeared. However, its main feature, a most impressive five-arched

The Thames and Severn Canal

In 1779 a short canal was opened between Stroud and the River Severn. Quickly successful, the Stroudwater became a busy carrier of coal and wool, and so its shareholders were encouraged to invest in another, associated venture, a canal from Stroud to the Thames near Lechlade. Opened in 1789, this offered a direct route from Thames to Severn, and it became the first of the cross-country waterways of southern England to be completed. Next came the Wilts & Berks and then the Kennet & Avon. Logically the Thames & Severn should have been a great success, but it was plagued by problems of water supply and poor engineering. Furthermore, it was built with narrow locks, and so the broad barges using the Thames, the Severn and the Stroudwater had to tranship their loads onto smaller boats.

As a result, through traffic was always irregular, and by 1911 it had all ceased. Although the Stroudwater remained in use until the 1940s, the Thames & Severn was derelict before 1920. Dramatically engineered, amid fine Cotswold scenery, and with distinctive architecture, notably the circular lock-keepers' cottages, the Thames & Severn is an attractive waterway, easily explored on foot or by car. Since the 1970s it has been a candidate for full restoration and, along with the Stroudwater, is being gradually rebuilt with the aim of being re-opened to navigation. There are many difficulties, not least the massive Sapperton tunnel, 3,808yds long, with splendid portals, but partially collapsed deep under the Cotswolds. However, the reopening of the Kennet & Avon has shown that such seemingly impossible tasks can be successfully accomplished.

Above: *Entrance to Sapperton tunnel at Coates on the disused Thames & Severn Canal.*

179

stone aqueduct, built to take the canal across the Torridge, still survives, now carrying the drive to a local mansion.

The Wilts and Berks Canal

A truly forgotten waterway, the Wilts & Berks is the least familiar and the least visible of the canals of southern England. Opened in 1810 to link the Kennet & Avon Canal with the Thames, it followed a remarkably indirect and meandering route from Semington to Abingdon across the flat landscape. It had over 40 locks, but no other engineering features of note, a number of branches, serving Calne, Chippenham and Wantage, and a link with the Thames & Severn via the North Wilts Canal. The network totalled over 65 miles, and the main cargo was coal from the Somerset fields, which kept the canal reasonably busy until the 1870s. All traffic had ceased by the early 20th century, and the canal was formally abandoned in 1914. Since then much of its route has disappeared, particularly in the towns. However, in the rural regions there is plenty of the Wilts &

Above: *Rolle Aqueduct on the derelict Torrington Canal.*

Berks to be found, and some sections have even been rescued from quiet oblivion and repaired. Complete restoration is, however, out of the question, and so it is an ideal waterway for those who enjoy digging up obscure corners of British industrial history with the aid of an Ordnance Survey map.

The Worcester and Birmingham Canal

Authorised by Parliament in 1791, the Worcester & Birmingham was planned as a rival to the Staffordshire & Worcestershire Canal, with a more direct route from the Severn to Birmingham. With the long tunnel at King's Norton, and its 58 locks in 30 miles, it was an expensive canal to build, and the

Left: *Tardebigge locks on the Worcester & Birmingham Canal.*

route was not fully open until 1815. Successful and busy in its heyday with a wide range of cargoes, the canal was an early victim of direct railway competition, and by 1864 was in financial difficulties. Sold in 1874 to the Sharpness New Docks Company, it was, in effect, subsidised by the Gloucester & Sharpness Canal for the rest of its commercial life. A candidate for closure during the 1950s, it was saved by leisure boating, and it is now a much-loved waterway despite the hard work involved in the 30-lock Tardebigge flight. The canal joins the Severn in the heart of Worcester, via a series of basins right by the cathedral, and the route into Birmingham is full of interest and surprisingly rural.

CENTRAL ENGLAND AND WALES

The Ashby Canal
Today the Ashby Canal seems little more than a 22-mile branch of the Coventry, yet when it received its parliamentary assent in 1794 it was conceived as a grand waterway to link the Coventry Canal, and thus the Midlands, to the Trent at Burton. As with the Coventry, coal was its inspiration, and indeed remained the major traffic on the canal until the 1960s. The section from Bosworth to Moira was completed by 1802, but this long, lock-free stretch proved to be as far as the canal reached. The next section, from Moira to the Trent, was never even started because of the prohibitive cost of the engineering involved. The Ashby's route, which now ends at Snarestone, the 8-mile section from here to Moira having been closed by mining subsidence, is particularly rural, passing a series of attractive villages and the site of the Battle of Bosworth Field. Another claim to fame was the town of Measham near Moira, whose potteries supplied boating families with the famous large and decorative barge teapots.

The Bridgewater Canal
The first modern canal in Britain, the Bridgewater was engineered by James Brindley and opened in 1761. Its patron and instigator, the 3rd Duke of Bridgewater, commissioned it to carry coal from his mines near Worsley to Manchester. Considerably expanded over the next century and connected by branches to other waterways, the Bridgewater was immensely successful, with commercial traffic continuing until the 1970s. The 28-mile route from Castlefield Junction in the heart of Manchester to Runcorn has no locks. Its canal connections include the Rochdale, in Manchester, the Leeds & Liverpool via the Leigh branch, the Trent & Mersey at Preston Brook, and the Manchester Ship Canal. It was the building of the Ship Canal in the early 1890s that gave the Bridgewater its most famous feature, the great Barton swing aqueduct, an iron trough that swings on its central axis to allow the passage of vessels using the Ship Canal. It replaced a masonry aqueduct over the River Irwell, the first such structure built in Britain and frequently illustrated in 18th-century engravings as a modern wonder.

The Coventry Canal
Although in itself not a major waterway, the Coventry Canal was one of the most profitable in Britain, regularly paying a dividend to shareholders up to nationalisation in 1947. When authorised by Parliament in 1768 the canal had two aims, first to supply Coventry with coal from the Bedworth field, and second to connect Coventry to the Trent & Mersey Canal. The first was quickly realised but the second was not achieved until 1790, owing to various disputes and financial problems. Because of its links with other waterways, such as the Oxford and Grand Junction canals, the Coventry was quickly successful and, once its connection with the Trent & Mersey was finally achieved, it became a vital link in the expanding network of the Midlands. This was the reason for its continued success. Its route, while not dramatic, is pleasant, and Coventry still boasts an active canal basin at its heart.

The Derby and Nottingham Canals
The Erewash Canal, running north from the River Trent for 12 miles to Langley Mill, became at the end of the 18th century the backbone of a local waterway network. The Cromford Canal joined it from the north, from the northwest came the short Nutbrook Canal, built to serve the coal mines and iron works between Ilkeston and Trowell, from the west came the Derby Canal, and on the east there was the Nottingham Canal. Today all these connections have largely disappeared, and only the Erewash remains in use. The Derby Canal, opened in 1796, was a 13-mile loop that linked Derby to the Erewash, and to the Trent & Mersey to the south at Swarkestone. Coal was the primary cargo, and the canal remained profitable throughout the 19th century. Its most important engineering feature was the cast iron Holmes aqueduct, designed by Benjamin Outram and probably the first to be made of this material in the world. Along with most of the route, this has disappeared, for the canal, unusually in private ownership until its end, was closed in 1964 and progressively obliterated. Today, Derby is one of the few of Britain's major towns without a waterway link. The Nottingham Canal was built to offer boats a more direct route into the city from the Cromford Canal. It ran from Langley Mill for about 14 miles to join the Trent in Nottingham. Predominantly industrial in its surroundings, it was busy until the early years of this century, and then a steady decline led to abandonment in 1937. Today, parts of the route survive to be explored, particularly around Eastwood, the birthplace of D H Lawrence. Nottingham is, of course, still accessible by boat via the River Trent navigation.

Left: *Langley Mill Basin on the Erewash Canal.*

The Grantham Canal

One of the best preserved of England's disused waterways is the Grantham Canal, running from the Trent at West Bridgford to Grantham, with a wandering 33-mile route across the Vale of Belvoir. Entirely rural, and with no major engineering features, the canal always had a river-like quality, and its route can easily be followed both on the map and on the ground. It was opened in 1797, traded profitably until it was taken over by a railway company in the mid-19th century, and then declined slowly until its final closure in 1936. Although short sections have disappeared, the Grantham Canal has always been a possible candidate for restoration. Its route is in any case a pleasant walk and a way to bring to life the frenetic enthusiasm for waterways in the late 18th century, when even quite small market towns were able to raise enough money to build their own canals.

Above: *A peaceful scene on the Grantham Canal.*

The Shropshire Union Canal

The Shropshire Union Railways and Canal Company was formed in 1846 from a merger of several independent canals, and rapidly grew to become one of the largest waterway networks in Britain. At its peak the tentacles of this empire stretched from Wolverhampton in the south to Ellesmere Port in the north, and westwards to Shrewsbury, Coalport and Ironbridge, Llangollen and Newtown, Montgomery. However, its backbone was the 66-mile main line from Autherley on the Staffordshire & Worcestershire Canal to Chester and Ellesmere Port, built by three separate companies between 1774 and 1835. Many of the branches have been lost, but this main line, after a long and successful

Left: *Rural moorings near Beeston, Cheshire, on the Shropshire Union Canal.*

commercial life, is still one of the most popular cruising waterways in Britain. The southern part of the route, from Autherley to Nantwich, was engineered by Telford and is characterised by its straight line, maintained by deep cuttings, by narrow locks grouped in flights, and by embankments and iron aqueducts over the A5 near Brewood and the A51 at Nantwich. The northern part, from Nantwich to Chester and on to Ellesmere Port, is a much older canal with broad locks, crossing attractive wooded countryside. The canal's passage through Chester is dramatic and there is a short arm connecting it to the River Dee. The terminus at Ellesmere Port, a creation of the canal company and until the 1940s the busiest canal port in Britain, has locks connecting it to the Manchester Ship Canal, and thus to the sea. After years of decay the port has been restored, and now houses the Boat Museum.

The Trent and Mersey Canal

Built between 1766 and 1777, with James Brindley as its engineer until his death in 1772, the Trent & Mersey was conceived as the first of a series of canals to link the major rivers of England. Its route, from the Bridgewater Canal at Preston Brook to the Trent Navigation at Shardlow, was a spectacular feat of engineering, including as it does 76 locks, some broad, but the majority narrow, aqueducts and a series of tunnels. It was these, the first to be dug in Britain, that made the canal famous in the 18th century. The longest, 2,879yds through Harecastle Hill near Stoke-on-Trent, took 11 years to construct. Popularly known as the Grand Trunk Canal, the Trent & Mersey had as one of its main promoters the potter Josiah Wedgwood, and its route as a result passed right by his new factory at Etruria. Coal, salt, and pottery materials were the primary cargoes on what became, in commercial terms, a highly profitable waterway, with continued success ensured by its connections

with a number of other waterways, including the River Weaver, and the Macclesfield, Caldon, Staffordshire & Worcestershire and Coventry canals. The most remarkable of these is at Anderton, where the junction with the Weaver is achieved by a vertical boat lift, a unique piece of canal engineering built in 1875. The landscape of the Trent & Mersey is interesting and varied as it crosses the Cheshire Plain, climbs up through 32 locks to the Harecastle summit, 408ft above sea level, and then descends through wooded and rolling countryside to the Trent Valley and

Above: *Unrestored lock on the Montgomery Canal, once part of the extensive Shropshire Union Railways & Canal Company.*

Derbyshire. Once heavily industrialised, and flanked by salt and coal mines, pottery factories and breweries, the route is now more rural, although enough industry survives in towns like Middlewich, Stoke-on-Trent and Burton-on-Trent to give a flavour of the canal's history.

Right: *Anderton boat lift on the Trent & Mersey.*

Weight limit
10T per axle

THE NORTH OF ENGLAND

The Chesterfield Canal

Planned by James Brindley, who did not live to see it finished, the 46-mile Chesterfield Canal was opened in 1777 from West Stockwith on the Trent to Chesterfield. The route included 65 locks and a very long tunnel at Norwood. The industries of the Chesterfield area, notably the coal and lead mines, benefited directly from the opening of the canal, which was soon busy, and at its peak in the 1840s the waterway was carrying 200,000 tons a year. In railway ownership from 1848, the canal suffered increasingly from mining subsidence, and in 1908 a major collapse in the Norwood tunnel permanently closed the canal's upper reaches and isolated Chesterfield itself. Much of this section has since disappeared, but parts of the route can be explored on foot through attractive, wooded countryside. The southern 25-mile section, from Worksop to the Trent, has remained open, even though commercial traffic ceased in the 1950s, and is now popular with pleasure cruisers owing to the varied and interesting nature of the landscape and the presence on the route of attractive places such as Wiseton and Retford. Nearby is Sherwood Forest, and all around are the parks and mansions of the Dukeries.

The Fossdyke Canal and Witham Navigation

The Fossdyke was built by the Romans, and so is easily the oldest artificial waterway in Britain that is still in use. It was constructed to link the River Trent to the River Witham in Lincoln, another Roman navigation, and was subsequently used by the Danes and the Normans, and through the Middle Ages. A typical cargo was stone for Lincoln Cathedral. Virtually derelict by the 17th century, the Fossdyke was extensively improved during

Above: *Lock gates on the Chesterfield Canal.*

the 18th century, and trade returned. At the same time the building of the Grand Sluice at Boston in 1766 protected the lock-free waterways from the adverse effects of tides. Further improvements followed during the 19th century, notably widening and straightening of the route, often in connection with local drainage schemes. In 1846 the two waterways were taken over by a railway company, and trade then declined steadily. In this century their isolation and the distinctive quality of their landscape have given them a new lease of life for pleasure cruising. Straight and lock-free, the Fossdyke runs from Torksey on the Trent to Lincoln where it meets the Witham. This navigation, more canal than river, then continues on to Boston,

a total of 43 miles. The highlights of the waterways are the quiet villages along the route, the memorable vista of the Lincolnshire landscape, and Lincoln and Boston, two of Britain's best waterway towns.

The Lancaster Canal

A grand waterway planned by John Rennie, the Lancaster Canal was inspired by the need to link Lancaster to the national network. The chosen route was from Kendal to near Wigan, and work began in 1792. There were to be only 8 locks, in a flight at Tewitfield, and major aqueducts crossing the Lune and the Ribble. By 1799 the canal was open from Preston to Tewitfield, with the great Lune aqueduct, a typically elegant Rennie design, and in the south from Clayton to Chorley. In cooperation with the Leeds & Liverpool Canal, who shared part of the southern section, it was later extended to Wigan, while in the north it was opened to Kendal in 1819. The only problem remained the 5-mile section in the middle, which included the crossing of the Ribble. In 1803 this was bridged by a 'temporary' tramway, but in the event the canal link was never completed, and so the northern section of the Lancaster was doomed to be isolated for ever. In 1826 a branch was opened to the sea at Glasson Dock, giving the northern section access to a port. With its original length of 75 miles, the Lancaster is remarkable for its lack of locks, and its route represents a major achievement in engineering terms. It also enabled the canal company to operate express fly boat services between Preston and Kendal, which transported passengers in the 1820s at an average speed of 10 miles per hour. Shortage of traffic on the northern section resulted in a steady closure from Kendal downwards from the 1930s, and in 1968 the whole section north from Tewitfield, including the flight of locks, was abandoned after the canal had been cut by the M6 motorway. From Preston southwards the canal remains open, and provides an unusual introduction to Lakeland scenery. The northern section, still largely in good condition, offers a most enjoyable towpath walk.

The Rochdale and Huddersfield Narrow Canals

The two great restoration dreams that have gripped canal enthusiasts for decades are the two lost trans-Pennine waterways, the Rochdale and the Huddersfield Narrow. Work on the former progresses steadily, but the sight of boats navigating the full length of the latter must be years away. In engineering terms these waterways were among the greatest triumphs of the canal age. The Rochdale, planned by William Jessop, was a

Above: *The Waterwitch pub on the Lancaster Canal.*

major undertaking, a broad canal with 92 locks in its 33 miles from Castlefields, Manchester, where it joined the Bridgewater Canal to Sowerby Bridge, where it met the Calder & Hebble. Like its other trans-Pennine rivals, the Rochdale was initially successful as a cross-country waterway link, but increasingly from the mid-19th century the traffic was localised at the two ends, with the Manchester canals remaining busy well into this century. The lack of through traffic resulted in slipping standards of maintenance and much of the Rochdale had become impassable by the 1940s. In 1952 it was formally closed. The route is dramatic, both in the cavernous passage through the towns that flank the canal and in the climb to the summit between Todmorden and Rochdale across a landscape of spectacular grandeur. The route is easily followed throughout, and provides a

memorable towpath walk filled with the ghosts of the Industrial Revolution. This is the best way to enjoy the Rochdale until boats can once again face the daunting 56-lock climb between Castlefields and the summit.

Just as exhilarating a towpath walk is the route of the Rochdale's great rival, the Huddersfield Narrow Canal. With 74 locks in a little over 20 miles and the longest canal tunnel in Britain, the Huddersfield can claim to be one of the most exciting waterways in Britain, reflecting both the extraordinary achievement of the canal navvies who carved it out of Pennine rock, and the challenge it presented to the boats using it. Opened in 1811, its route was from the Ashton Canal near Manchester to Huddersfield, where it met the broad canal that then led to the Calder & Hebble. Its narrow locks carried it up to 656ft above sea level, by far the highest

Above: *The Huddersfield Narrow Canal at Uppermill.*

summit level in Britain. On the summit is Standedge Tunnel, 5,698yds long, and cut yard by yard through solid gritstone at a cost of £160,000. Never a commercial success and an early victim of railway competition, with the first of the three lines that ran in parallel tunnels through Standedge being opened in 1847, the canal was soon in railway ownership. Trans-Pennine traffic had ceased by the early years of this century, and one of the last through passages along the canal was made by L C T Rolt in 1940. It was formally abandoned in 1944, but much of the route still survives in good condition as it is used as a water supply channel. Like the other trans-Pennine waterways, the Huddersfield Narrow Canal brings to life in the most dramatic way the extraordinary imagination and dynamic ambition of the canal engineers and the teams of navvies that brought their schemes to fruition. The restoration of the Huddersfield Narrow would be a worthy monument to their magnificent achievement.

The Sheffield and South Yorkshire Navigation

One of the few waterways in Britain to have been rebuilt to international standards, the Sheffield & South Yorkshire is a modern and commercial canal with large, automated locks. Yet, its history is much older, for at its heart is the River Don, used as a navigation at least since the Middle Ages. From the early 18th century this river navigation was steadily improved and extended, to Rotherham by 1740 and to Tinsley, south of Sheffield, ten years later. Coal was the primary cargo, with the waterway serving a number of fields previously accessible only by land. In 1804 the Dearne & Dove Canal provided a link with Barnsley, a busy waterway until its final abandonment in 1961. More important was the Stainforth & Keadby Canal, built in the 1790s to bypass the dangerous waters of the River Don. This inspired the development of a major port at Keadby, on the Trent. By 1820 the navigation had also been extended from Tinsley to the heart of Sheffield. A period of railway ownership followed, and then all the separate components were grouped together as the Sheffield & South Yorkshire Navigation, a 43-mile route from Keadby to Sheffield, with various branches. In 1905 the opening of the New Junction Canal linked it with the Aire & Calder and gave direct access to the port of Goole. The coalfields and industry of the Don Valley have ensured the continued commercial success of these canals to the present day, and so Doncaster and Sheffield can still claim to be genuine centres of inland waterway activity.

SCOTLAND

The Crinan Canal

A particularly delightful waterway, the 9-mile Crinan Canal was built from Ardrishaig on Loch Gilp to Crinan on the Sound of Jura to enable sea-going vessels to avoid the 132-mile route round the Mull of Kintyre. Opened in 1809 and equipped with 15 locks, and a number of swing bridges, the Crinan is surrounded by spectacular scenery, clinging to the loch side and rocky shore line at each end and cutting through the steep hills that mark the peninsula's narrow neck. There are attractive little harbours at Ardrishaig and Crinan, filled with an interesting variety of fishing boats and pleasure craft. While never a great commercial success, the Crinan is still a busy waterway, and its 20ft wide locks are big enough for most of the modern boats likely to use it. All the major Scottish canals, the Crinan, the Caledonian and the Forth & Clyde, were built without fixed bridges, to allow the passage of vessels with tall masts. On the Crinan, crews open the bridges themselves, an activity enjoyed by spectators on the towpath, which is in itself an excellent walk.

Above: *Crinan Basin on the Crinan Canal.*

The Edinburgh and Glasgow Union Canal

Opened in 1822, this fine waterway was built to enable boats to travel from Glasgow to Edinburgh, via its link with the Forth & Clyde Canal at Port Downie, near Falkirk. The connection between the two canals was made by an impressive flight of 11 locks, destroyed when traffic on the Edinburgh & Glasgow Union ceased in the early 1930s. After years of gradual decay, the canal was formally abandoned in 1965. Until the opening of the Edinburgh & Glasgow Railway in 1842, the canal was famous for its passenger services. Although sections of the waterway have been re-opened, complete restoration is unlikely. However, most of its attractive route can be followed and still surviving are the Union's three great aqueducts, larger and more impressive than most south of the border. The

most famous is the 12-arch structure that carries the canal for over 800ft high above the valley of the Avon. The other two, over the River Almond between Broxburn and Ratho, and over the Water of Leith at Slateford, are both well over 400ft long.

The Forth and Clyde Canal

Until its sudden closure in 1962, the Forth & Clyde Canal was a popular and well-used route, linking Scotland's east and west coasts. The 35-mile route, opened in 1790, from Bowling Harbour, on the Clyde in Glasgow, to Grangemouth on the east coast, had 39 locks, and a range of other interesting engineering features, the most important of which, the grand four-arched stone aqueduct over the River Kelvin near Glasgow, still stands as a constant reminder of the canal's

Above: *The Forth & Clyde Canal near Kirkintilloch.*

potential. Built in 1790, this was long considered to be one of the best such structures in Britain. Nearby is the remains of the short arm that linked the canal to Glasgow city centre, now traceable as far as Port Dundas. Originally it continued to Parkston Basin, where there was a junction with the 12-mile Monkland Canal, opened in 1793 to supply Glasgow with coal from Airdrie and to serve the iron industry of Coatbridge. The Forth & Clyde was planned by the engineer John Smeaton, and it was probably he who chose the unusual lock size of 68ft by just under 20ft, often criticised for being too small. Despite this, trade continued on the canal well into this century, and there was traffic right up to the closure. It was a well-built canal, with a long summit level and flights of locks at each end, often with unusual hand-operated features. The Forth & Clyde is now subject to a major restoration scheme and parts are already back in use. One hopes that the short term thinking that provoked its closure will be reversed one day when boats can once again sail across Scotland from Forth to Clyde.

Right: *Veteran steam puffer in the lock at Ardrishaig on the Crinan Canal.*

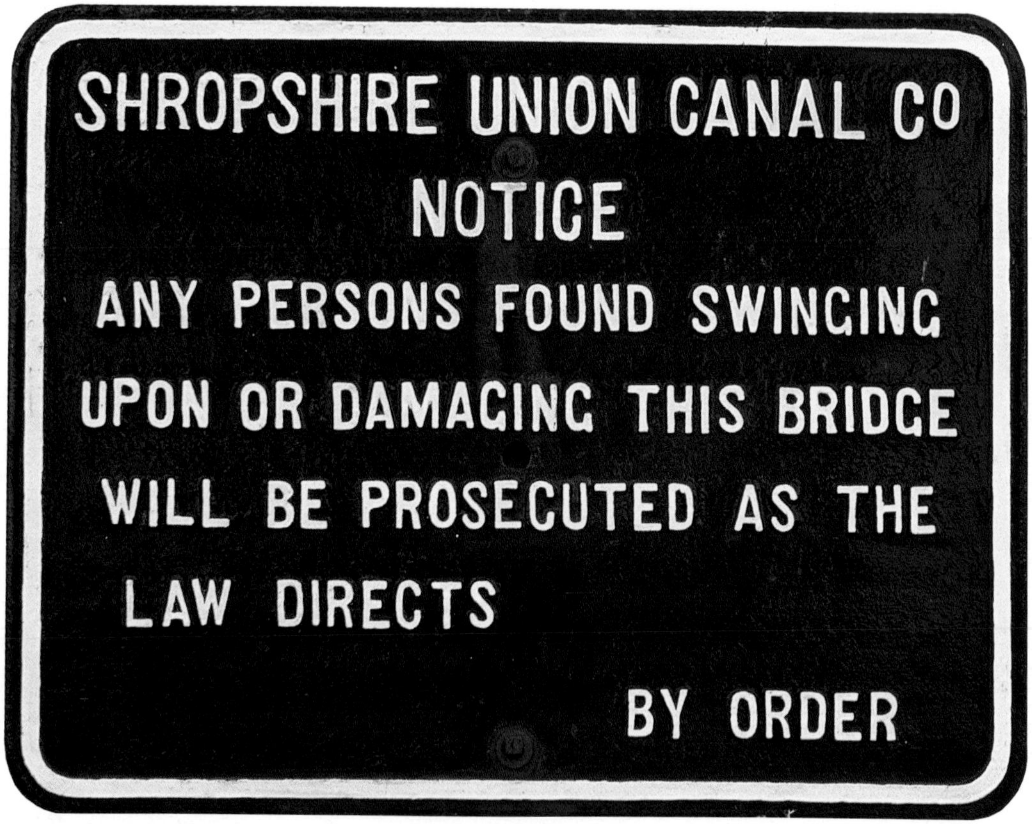

SHROPSHIRE UNION CANAL C̱O̱

NOTICE

ANY PERSONS FOUND SWINGING

UPON OR DAMAGING THIS BRIDGE

WILL BE PROSECUTED AS THE

LAW DIRECTS

BY ORDER